I Know You're in There

A Memoir of loss, healing, farming, and adventure

GRACE HERNANDEZ

BALBOA.
PRESS
A DIVISION OF HAY HOUSE

Balboa Press books may be ordered through booksellers or by contacting:

Balboa Press
A Division of Hay House
1663 Liberty Drive
Bloomington, IN 47403
www.balboapress.com
1 (877) 407-4847

Because of the dynamic nature of the Internet, any web addresses or links contained in this book may have changed since publication and may no longer be valid. The views expressed in this work are solely those of the author and do not necessarily reflect the views of the publisher, and the publisher hereby disclaims any responsibility for them.

The author of this book does not dispense medical advice or prescribe the use of any technique as a form of treatment for physical, emotional, or medical problems without the advice of a physician, either directly or indirectly. The intent of the author is only to offer information of a general nature to help you in your quest for emotional and spiritual well-being. In the event you use any of the information in this book for yourself, which is your constitutional right, the author and the publisher assume no responsibility for your actions.

Any people depicted in stock imagery provided by Thinkstock are models, and such images are being used for illustrative purposes only.
Certain stock imagery © Thinkstock.

Photo credit to Jamie McConnell for Author photo on the back cover of the book.

Print information available on the last page.

ISBN: 978-1-4525-9086-8 (sc)
ISBN: 978-1-4525-9088-2 (hc)
ISBN: 978-1-4525-9087-5 (e)

Library of Congress Control Number: 2014900930

Balboa Press rev. date: 10/09/2019

For Auntie Jo, thank you for your sense of humor!

"Out beyond ideas of wrongdoing and rightdoing
there is a field. I'll meet you there." --Rumi

Contents

Part Three

Part Four

Acknowledgements

Being a seeker, I've had the privilege of meeting incredible people. People who live with their hearts open. One person in particular is my husband. Michael, you amaze me and inspire me! Co-creating with you has been the greatest gift of my life. Your patience, devotion and conviction for a joyous life are the torches that have carried me through uncertain times. You are the love of my life. I appreciate who you are.

My Aunt Jo was insistent about me writing a book. Whenever she would mention it, I would balk at the commitment. How could I ever sit that still? After our adventures at Buxton Farm, I took Aunt Jo's advice to heart. I love you Jo.

The list of people who have touched my life in profound and simple ways is endless. Most of you know who you are. A big thanks to all of you for teaching me there's strength in vulnerability.

Chelsey Shannon: For your friendship, your courage, independent nature and writer's advice. I admire your talent.

Katherine Boone: For being consistently optimistic and for your gentle critiques, advice and timely edits.

Valerie Valentine: For your proofreading skills, professional guidance and your commitment to keep the momentum going.

To Mom: For the laughter, tears and friendship.

To Dad: For inspiring me to write and for teaching me to let go.

To my sisters: For all the incredible memories and for being my big sisters!

To my brother Brian: For sharing your passion for music with me.

To my nephews: For your courage in following your heart wherever it takes you.

To Gary David: For inspiring me to share my life experiences.

To Margie Bushman and Wesley Roe from Santa Barbara Permaculture Network: For your unwavering commitment to sustainability.

To Joel Salatin: For your infectious spirit.

To Micki Cabaniss at Grateful Steps Publishing: For your direction.

To Cecil Bothwell: For planting the seed.

To Susan Hurt, Amanda Rodriguez, and Richard VanDeventer at Balboa Press: For making this happen.

To the reader: For following the impulse to read my story.

To Mother Nature: For restoring my health.

To unseen forces: For guiding me every step of the way.

To the collective conscious: For our ability to heal no matter what.

I Know You're In There

_____

Part One

Fifteen Minutes

Friday June 29th 2011 was a gorgeous summer day without a cloud in the sky. We finished our daily workload ahead of schedule, so we sent our apprentice Alec home early and looked forward to a quiet weekend to ourselves. My first priority that weekend was to rest my injured foot. After chores, we came in and ate dinner. I was doing the dishes and listening to our local Alleghany Mountain Radio Station. The DJ was caught off guard because winds kept forcing the door to his studio open. The strength of the winds bewildered him.

Michael had a routine of tracking the weather, and the forecast was clear that morning. I knew weather patterns often came from West Virginia, and in those mountains, weather could change in a heartbeat. Something odd and forewarning was coming from the radio. Within seconds, the sky turned black, and the wind abruptly picked up. Michael and I bolted out of the farmhouse. We had fifteen minutes to get to three hundred head of cattle, two geese and five hundred laying hens two miles down the road.

As we blazed our way down Buxton's driveway, we drove past our car which was parked under a large oak tree in our front yard. We had no time to consider our home, our tiny studio, or our safety. Beautiful trees paralleling our driveway swayed and groaned above us. Winds were so fierce that for a second, we thought we were in a tornado. Our little farm truck was almost lifted off the driveway with both of us in it. It was a scene from The Wizard of Oz. Being the practical man he is, Michael thought we should turn around, but it was already too late; trees fell like paperclips toward the earth, blocking our route home. We could only go forward.

As soon as we got to the herd, lightning struck, and a few trees toppled over. We watched the cows scramble off the hilltop. They sounded like a herd of elephants as they rumbled through the field and down to the valley below. They broke through one fence line after another to get to lower ground and cried out in agitation, but there was nothing we could do; our lives were now at risk in the open field. I was amazed at their instincts; they knew exactly what to do to save themselves. Why didn't we?

In the pasture, gates fell off their hinges, rain pelted us, and lightning struck over and over. We threw the geese in the back of the truck, captured every hen in sight and locked them up inside their eggmobile. The cows were on their own. It was clear to us their survival instincts were intact.

We got to the gate and my heart raced with anticipation. If we didn't get to safe ground soon, we could easily lose our lives on that open road. We only knew two neighbors, and one lived directly across the field we were in, but his home was dark and uninviting. Carl and Norma lived about another mile down the road, risking the drive to their house wasn't appealing, but it was our only option.

The geese squealed in our open bed truck as we edged our way through the steep S-curves. Tree branches slammed down around us. Michael slowed his speed around each tight curve. There wasn't another car in sight. Carl and Norma's house was dark, but they motioned from the door for us to come in. I felt a pinch of relief inside their home. For the moment, we were in good hands.

They informed us that Dave, one of the Buxton Farm owners, was visiting for the weekend, so I called the main house and asked him to move our car away from the tree and close up the windows of our tiny studio. The thought of losing the only two things we owned in that storm was deeply disturbing.

Norma and Carl had the emergency weather radio station on, and the reporter gave full reports of the severity of the storm. My mind wandered back to our thousand broilers in the open pasture; by then, the wind had surely destroyed them. We had just put our turkey poults out that morning, and with the speed of the wind, I knew their pens had probably blown apart. We couldn't get home to rescue any of them.

Sitting at Carl and Norma's kitchen table, on the edge of panic, my entire body was on high alert, racing with adrenaline. Inside I trembled. I was offered water, respite, but I couldn't sit still. I felt an overwhelming desire to get back to the farm, to our animals, and our personal belongings. But how?

Once the storm backed off a bit, Carl and Michael devised a plan to get us home. I didn't see how it was possible with so many trees down, but Carl wasn't intimidated. He took the lead in his old green truck and we followed closely behind. The country road was dark, isolated, and full of danger. Trees flexed into back bends and then broke as we made our way over the CowPasture River. Below, the river roared with unbelievable force.

Carl handled his chainsaw with precision and without pausing, he cut through tree after tree blocking our path. Michael and I followed him, casting large pine, walnut, and oak trees to the side of the road. Inch by inch, we made our way down the windy path that barely resembled a country road. Every few seconds, I gazed above us to make certain that additional wounded trees didn't tumble down upon us; their reaction to the violent wind was totally unpredictable.

In his seventies, Carl was still solid and strong. He knew that land like the back of his hand. When he was ten years old, his parents left him and his older brother alone one winter. The two boys dropped out of school and learned how to hunt for food. They fended for themselves during a cold lonely season. There weren't too many of these old-timers left in that neck of the woods. His commitment to get us home safely was relentless. You want a person like him at your side in a storm this severe.

Finally, a path to the farmhouse was visible. When I noticed our car was in the same spot under the large oak tree, my stomach rumbled. I neglected to tell Dave how to start our electric car. The hood was caved in with a large branch. I jumped out of our truck and tried moving it before any further damage could occur, but it was blocked by limbs as big as full-grown trees in front and back.

There were five hundred chicks in our poultry brooder waiting patiently for warmth. In a corner, they huddled tightly together. I turned their propane heaters on and closed them up. With the grid down, they had no water.

Outside the door to the brooder was where we processed and stored our poultry and eggs. Refrigerators were blown over and bright orange yolks spilled across the white cement. Freezers loaded with our latest poultry harvest started to defrost.

We headed out to the broiler field to check on our poultry. Some of the pens were demolished and birds were discarded in the open field. We put at least fifty turkey poults out that morning; all of them were dead. There was no sign of our guard dog, Jack. He was very sensitive to thunder and lightning, and a storm that size surely sent him running. By the time we arrived at our tiny studio, it was past midnight. Fortunately Dave had secured our windows. Miraculously our tiny studio was still intact. Disoriented and exhausted, we collapsed into slumber.

Polyface Farm, Swoope, Virginia

When Joel Salatin came to Santa Barbara to participate in The Carbon Farming Series Workshop, I signed up for two days and I was immediately impressed with his friendly, enthusiastic personality. He was eager to share his experiences about his family farm, Polyface Farm, in Swoope, Virginia. He inspired me to make a few improvements with the poultry on our homestead. At that time, we raised and butchered chickens and a few ducks for ourselves and a few friends, but after the workshop, I decided to add turkeys to the mix!

During the workshop, Joel also shared how past apprentices were managing a few of his rental or satellite farms. Unknowingly, that weekend, he planted a few seeds in my mind about the possibility of stewarding land. By the end of the workshop, I understood clearly he carried his farm with him wherever he went. His "can-do" attitude lit another fire inside of me. I went home and for the first time looked at his Polyface Farms website. The thought of somehow joining his team appealed to me.

A few months later I was at a seed saving exchange in Santa Barbara when I learned Polyface Farm held summer workshops. I thought it would be a great idea to see their farm firsthand. When I told Michael about the workshop, he said, "Sign us up!" So I did. Six months later we combined our family visit to Ohio with a trip to Virginia to attend The Polyface Intensive Discovery Seminar.

The drive from the Midwest to the South was stunning. Lush green pastures and vast open spaces in Virginia were a welcomed change. Rivers flowed and traffic was light. The summer humidity was intense, but after living in a dry climate for so long, it felt good to have moisture in our skin again.

We arrived in Staunton, Virginia and immediately felt welcomed. The Southern charm in that small town quickly caught our attention. We browsed through family-owned shops and ate a light breakfast at a locally owned restaurant. I could hardly wait to attend the seminar the following day. With so much anticipation, we checked into our hotel and slept like babies.

When we pulled up to Polyface Farm for breakfast the following day, Joel's mother, Lucille, greeted us. She was friendly and very helpful. I don't know why I was amazed she was working the event, but I was. It was hardly 7:00 a.m. and she was sharp as a whistle. Her genuine personality impressed me.

After breakfast, Daniel Salatin, Joel's son, butchered a rabbit. He performed that task with the perfection of a master, if I had blinked, I would have missed it. We were introduced to all the things Joel talked about in the workshop I took with him in Santa Barbara. I reveled in seeing things firsthand. We saw the broiler pens, eggmobile, brooder, saw mill, rabbits, the Racken House where hens and rabbits live together, hoop houses where summer vegetables were growing, the farm store, and the lush pastures. Joel drove the group up the mountain in the hay wagon to visit the pigs. The pigs were running the show on top of that mountain. It was an dynamic arrangement that impressed all of us. While we were up there Joel demonstrated to the group how to cut down a tree. Clearly, it was one of his favorite outdoor activities on the farm. He made it look so easy. On our way down the mountain we stopped at various ponds they've built over the years. It was apparent to all of us that Joel loved his farm. His passionate storytelling about his parents purchasing the land was captivating.

Late afternoon on the second day of the workshop, Joel, Daniel, and interns took our group to move the herd at a satellite farm nearby. The scenery surrounding us was staggering; rolling hills and old farmhouses had distinct character. Joel motioned for all of us to stand in the middle of the pasture, and without any idea of what to expect, Daniel opened the gate and the herd barreled their way into the field to their next salad bar. Standing in between a few hundred unaggressive head of cattle was a rush. I loved every minute of it. Between the incredible sound of hundreds of cattle munching away and the fantastic scenery, there was a peacefulness in that setting that provoked a longing in me.

There were at least thirty people in the workshop. People from all walks of life. Some were already farming, some intending to farm, businessmen, homesteaders, students, East Coasters and West Coasters, even a woman in her seventies who was just starting her farm. I was in awe of her bravery. The range of stories and diverse backgrounds were impressive. All of us were eager to find ways to replicate, in some small way, what the Salatins were doing with their land and animals.

Before our trip to The Shenandoah Valley, I had no intention of falling in love with Virginia. In fact, the infatuation I felt toward Polyface Farm during that workshop was a total surprise to me. Yet, every time we passed a beautiful farm in the Shenandoah Valley, I felt a light tug at my heart. I voiced my unremitting desire to live in that beautiful setting to Michael, but his words quickly brought me back to reality: "We're not moving to Virginia. What in the world would we do here?"

I knew he was right, but for some unknown reason I felt drawn to that part of the country. The landscape, the home-cooked meals with Joel's family, the good-natured interns and apprentices, the variety of animals, life outdoors, the fertile landscape, even Michael the guard dog caught my attention that weekend. I think part of the allure was that many aspects of it reminded me of my Midwestern heritage.

The course was coming to an end, and I didn't want to leave. Our last meal together was outside on the lawn of the house, and it was fantastic. Before the workshop ended, Joel mentioned to the group that he had several farms with former apprentices managing them, and one of the farms needed a new farm manager. Being the great salesman he is, he caught the attention of several of us in the workshop. I listened closely as he spoke. He described some of the responsibilities of the farm manager and then presented the position to the group. Michael was sitting at another table, away from me, and I wondered if he too was feeling beckoned by Joel's proposal. We had been exploring other places and states to relocate to for at least a year, but none of those previous places we'd visited had the pull Virginia did that weekend. The beauty of the CommonWealth and the opportunity to work with Polyface seemed like a perfect combination for our next adventure.

As soon as Joel gave his blessing on the group and before I could even get to Michael, he was next to Joel inquiring about the position. He described our personal farm experiences, and he explained why we were interested in the satellite farm. Joel listened closely, then invited Michael to send more details in an email to Wendy, his store manager. It was a green light. Our desire to team up with Polyface was born that weekend. We soared back to Ohio.

Managing Buxton was exactly what we were looking for:stewardship of land and animals. The opportunity to farm full time with the Salatins seemed like the chance of a lifetime. Everything inside of us wanted that job. We talked about it to family and friends in Ohio with enthusiasm and joy. Then, we composed a sincere email and sent it off to Wendy, Joel's gatekeeper. We made our intentions clear; we were ready to work with Polyface Farms.

We drove to Cleveland to spend time with my dad's sister and our good friend, Aunt Jo. It had been a few years since we last saw her so we surprised her with an unannounced visit. She thought she was hallucinating when she saw us in her driveway. Our spontaneous visit made her weekend!

Aunt Jo was an entertainer, therapist, actress, comedian, writer and spiritual seeker, and a very powerful mentor to me and a good friend to Michael. We adored her. We shared our intention to work with Polyface Farm, and she was thrilled to know we might be living closer to her; the possibility filled her with joy. Spending time together lifted her spirits and ours. She was too weak to take to lunch, so we sat and visited with her for a long afternoon. One of the things I loved most about Aunt Jo was her sense of humor. She truly had a way of finding the irony in almost everything. In addition to her sense of humor, she was a great storyteller. We could listen to her for hours. I loved her enthusiasm and appreciated her support in our lives.

We left Cleveland and joined my immediate family back in Cincinnati. My dad was looking older and thinner, and his bald head was covered with cuts and burns from skin cancer treatments. All those years playing golf and swimming in the ocean caught up with him. He wore a baseball hat to cover the damage. He was 85 years old and still painted, swam, took walks, played cards, and sometimes golfed. He even rode one of my sister's horses that weekend. We cooked out just like the old days and enjoyed one final humid summer evening together before heading back to California. Spending time with my family was the perfect ending to an exceptional trip.

Back in California, my thoughts were mostly about Virginia. I had every intention of getting that job with Polyface Farms. I started visualizing life on that land. I imagined walking green pastures, moving the cows, collecting eggs from the chickens. I had no idea exactly what Buxton Farm looked like, but I imagined it and I daydreamed about us living on it. Deep within, I knew that job was for us. I casually mentioned to friends that we were considering working with Joel Salatin, but I didn't give it a lot of airtime because I didn't want anyone to influence my point of view in a negative way. And I certainly didn't want to hear the word "impossible." I was in a process that felt right, almost sacred, like I was summoning a new story, the next chapter in our lives. It took focus, intention, positive enthusiasm and an unwavering attitude.

Joel emailed us with a questionnaire, and we answered with eagerness and delight. I mentioned Permaculture design, King Hill Farm in Maine, and our homestead in Los Olivos, California. I described who we were and why we were the perfect couple for the position. One of the questions he asked was, "How long do you see yourself staying on the farm?" I remember joyfully answering, "Three years, five years, ten years." It felt right to respond with so much expectation and excitement. I was certain we were merging with something that would sustain us. Why wouldn't we want to stay forever?

We sent our answers to Joel and Daniel, and two weeks went by without a word. I suspected they were interviewing other families, so I waited patiently and continued to visualize. Then we got an email. Joel wondered if we could visit. It was all we needed: we booked our flights and responded yes, we would be there the following week. It was over Labor

Day weekend, which meant we would be celebrating Michael's birthday in Virginia. Perfect.

Two days before our return to Virginia, I got a call from someone who had a swarm of bees in their yard and she wanted them removed. At first it appeared to be an easy job, but during the process of retrieving them, it started getting dark. I quickly learned that working with bees at night wasn't fun. Without the sun as their navigator, they crawled all over me until one of them got inside my veil and stung me in the face. I was unable to remove the stinger until I got home, and by that time, my face was round, puffy, and inflamed. My entire head throbbed throughout the night. By the following morning, it had turned black and blue; I looked like an alien. It was impossible for me to go out into public. If the inflammation didn't reduce soon, I was sure we would have to cancel our trip to Virginia. Throughout the day I took ibuprofen for the pain and iced my face every twenty minutes. When we were ready to leave, most of the swelling was gone but not all of it. On the plane across the country, I continued to apply more ice. My compulsive efforts paid off, by the time we got to Virginia the swelling had dramatically decreased and I looked more like myself. What a relief!

Most people request a resume and references when they are considering you for a job. Not the Salatins. We liked their screening process. It was eye to eye, face to face. There was no place to hide. It was based on spending time together, listening to one another, sniffing each other out. For us, this approach worked. We were checking them out as much as they were checking us out.

We arrived for the interview at Polyface Farms in the early afternoon. Daniel Salatin took us inside the Salatin's farmhouse and described the position to us while Joel did a radio interview over the phone. Inside the old farmhouse with Daniel, Joel, and his wife Teresa, we were relaxed. It felt good to be back on their land. Outside, a team of apprentices moved about collecting eggs, moving cows, giving farm tours, and harvesting vegetables from various hoop houses. There was a palpable momentum on the farm.

We listened closely to Daniel's description of the job at Buxton. The farm manager was responsible for moving their herd of three hundred cattle every day, and following them with the eggmobile, which carried about six hundred hens. In exchange, Polyface paid the rent, phone and all utilities. There was no salary. Buxton Farm was close to a thousand acres, but we would be managing three hundred acres in pasture. To help us make money, Polyface offered us a market for eggs, broilers and turkeys. Depending on how much income we needed to make, we could raise as many as eight thousand broilers and a couple hundred turkeys. Polyface gave us the option of owning our poultry and creating our own market, or we could let them own everything, and then sell directly back to them. We were responsible for processing any poultry we raised.

We inquired about the previous farmer's abrupt departure. Apparently they had eight children, most of whom were homeschooled; the farm's remote setting was a challenge for their family. Also, instead of selling their broilers and eggs back to Polyface, they tried to establish their own market but the rural environment made this challenging. We listened closely to Daniel and concluded that if we managed Buxton we would start small and sell directly back to Polyface.

After Joel's radio interview, we drove with him out to Buxton Farm. It was the only satellite farm an hour away from Polyface, so we had plenty of time to discuss details. Michael and I skipped lunch in an effort to get to our interview on time, so I brought a few snacks to nibble on in the car. After opening a bag of gluten-free pretzels, I suddenly felt Joel didn't approve of me eating in the car. A few times he glanced over at me as I ruffled the bag of pretzels. I was certain Michael was rolling his eyes, watching me from the backseat. I was slightly nervous but since Joel didn't say anything, I carried on. However, I regretted not sitting in the backseat, that way I could have grazed without feeling self-conscious.

As Joel drove, we probed him with endless questions about Buxton. We tried to get a sense of how we would make money, where we would find people to help us butcher chickens, and how we would find apprentices to come to the farm. He was very open about what it took to manage Buxton Farm.

I had waited for weeks in anticipation of seeing what the farmhouse looked like. When we pulled up the driveway my first reaction was that it was rather strange looking, and not at all what I expected. I wasn't repulsed by it, or attracted to it. It simply wasn't my taste. But I immediately thought, "We can live there for a while."

Joel took us to the main house where the family that owned Buxton Farm stayed when they visited the farm. The house sat up on a hill and he was eager for us to see the view of the land. Wendy, the store manager at Polyface, had told us Buxton was exquisite and she was right. Our vision was filled with the main house overlooking the river, the turkeys in their feathernet, the herd of cows, Jack the guard dog, and all the empty broiler pens. We could see the pond, the manager's farmhouse, and the processing area, as well as the mountains and the George Washington National Forest that surrounds Buxton. The farm took our breath away.

We crossed the swinging bridge over the river to see the herd on the other side. The cables on that old bridge were weak and worn out. I trembled crossing it, because it swayed with every step I took. The cables looked like they might snap at any time, but after Joel walked across it without blinking, we followed. I wondered if successfully crossing that old bridge was part of our interview.

Once across, we met the herd and they were beautiful, but they were also extremely hot. We helped Matt, a Polyface apprentice temporarily living at Buxton Farm, get a confused, bloated calf up off the ground. Back across the river, we skipped rocks with Joel. The river was low, but the water looked pristine. It had been a long time since we'd seen a river so clear and clean.

Back at the farmhouse, we were joined by Kip, one of the landowners. She was friendly and eager to share Buxton Farm's history. The farm had been in the family since the 1940's, when her grandfather bought it. She spent summers riding horses and swimming in the river. Her parents lived on the farm full time until they died, then Kip and her two brothers, Dick and Dave, inherited the farm. Each of them had very fond memories growing up on the farm. They considered it their family treasure. It was an extraordinary piece of property with incredible potential. I marveled at the thought of inheriting a thousand acres.

Kip asked us how we felt about living in a rural environment, and assured us Bath County was nothing like the West Coast. The closest town didn't even have a stoplight. I could sense she considered the remoteness a concern, and I said, "At least we have Polyface." When I said that, Joel's reaction was something I will never forget. He looked away in the other direction, almost as if he said to himself, "Out here, dear, you'll be on your own." I took note of both of their reactions, but I wasn't in a position to hear anything that might challenge our desire to manage Buxton. I was certain we were meant to steward that land, and I didn't want anyone to influence us otherwise.

Before we left, we looked over the barnyard, the processing area, and the brooder. There were many old outbuildings, unused and abandoned: an old icehouse, root cellars, pig stalls and a beat-up henhouse. A ghostly feeling lingered on the farm. I couldn't put my finger on it. It was absolutely stunning and startling at the same time. Buxton needed so much love; I wondered if we were up to giving it.

On our drive back to Swoope, Joel wanted to know what our impressions were of Buxton, but it was impossible for me to give any feedback. I was overwhelmed by the scope and condition of the farm, and I needed time to take things in and process. I had no words yet, so I let Michael do the talking.

We arrived back at Polyface just in time to have dinner with the farm crew. Dan, the farm cook that season, prepared pulled pork from a pig that Daniel Salatin butchered earlier that week. It was tender, juicy and delicious. We shared conversation with Teresa and Lucille Salatin and the rest of the crew. It was less than two months after the workshop, and I was thrilled to be breaking bread again at Polyface in the beautiful Shenandoah Valley. The evening was warm and inviting. At that time of the day, the pace on the farm was slower. Michael and I gave appreciation for the great meal, and then went back to our hotel room and collapsed.

"Michael and I are driving along, we can't see the road ahead of us, and we keep driving until our car goes over the cliff into an abyss."

I woke up in the middle of the night, sweating after that dream. My subconscious was overwhelmed with doubt about Buxton Farm. Michael was also awake. After quietly sitting in the dark, we discussed some of our fears. Clearly, there were some concerns. Are we the right people for Buxton? What were we getting ourselves into? Is Buxton right for us? How will we make it work? How will we find people to help process thousands of broilers? What if the herd of three hundred cattle gets out at one time? Polyface is an hour away so who would help us catch them? Can we really butcher three hundred turkeys? They're so big and heavy. How do two people care for six hundred hens? All those eggs. We didn't know anyone in Virginia: would we be welcomed in that conservative neck of the woods? What about the size of Buxton? Can we shepherd a thousand acres? We were totally overwhelmed with doubt. We didn't know how we would manage the details, but I knew we would find a way.

The following morning, we returned to Polyface Farms. In order for us to establish an understanding about what it took to process hundreds of birds at Buxton, we needed to get our hands dirty, so we spent the next two hours with a crew of ten interns butchering about five hundred broilers. It was a flawless assembly line. Everyone was focused, and there were no glitches. It was a good decision to process broilers on our interview. It gave us insight into how it's done professionally: the timing, the right temperature of the scalder, the best kind of knives to use, how to extract pinfeathers. When all the details are covered, we agreed, it wasn't such a big deal after all. With the right amount of helping hands, we knew we could replicate what Polyface was doing.

Later in the afternoon, I was eating lunch when Joel strolled up to chat. He was curious to know how we were feeling about Buxton Farm. This time I didn't hold back. "Buxton needs a lot of love," I exclaimed. Joel looked at me as if I'd read his mind. I don't think he expected my observation to be that accurate. But it was true. We were thrilled to be considered for the position and Buxton was a gorgeous farm, but that old farm needed love, energy, attention, and devotion. It was in a desperate state; it needed someone to give a damn about it. It was a fact.

After processing the batch of broilers, we cleaned up and headed back to our hotel for a long nap. That evening we celebrated Michael's birthday at Zynodoa, a delicious local food restaurant in Staunton. It was the perfect ending to a life-changing weekend.

About two days after we returned to California we received an email from Joel.

Hi Michael and Grace--

Well, well, well. You did it. By unanimous acclamation of interns, apprentices, and the Salatins, we would be honored if you would accept the Buxton farm position on behalf of Polyface. You demonstrated the character and qualities we were looking for and would like to leverage that on the property there.

I trust your return home was uneventful--I know how far that is. I've done it many, many times and it never gets shorter. Here is what impressed us:

1. *You seemed very happy in your own skins. That means you don't need a lot of approval from others, you're happy together, and you're quite confident about your own ability to learn and grow with the landscape.*
2. *You understood the gravity of the situation. The kinds of questions you asked were deep and penetrating, showing that you grasped the whole task and the opportunity.*
3. *You pitched in, not only with the bloated calf, but with processing, when you could have held back. That is huge. You sized up the need of the moment, responded without inane questions or ignorant commentary, and jumped in as a meaningful part of the team. Wow!*
4. *You are stable--long marriage, successive projects, determined and slow progress toward the same basic goals for many years.*
5. *You are creative. We believe you will do things at Buxton we haven't even thought about, and will actually be a magnet for the community and others to lead by example. And that's the best kind of leadership. You*

are the only ones who immediately saw a potential greenhouse in the defunct and somewhat forlorn refrigerator framework. Whether you eventually redo that or tear it apart is inconsequential, but you clearly were looking at opportunities and thinking: utilization.

6. You were not enamored of the spectacular beauty of the place, but rather understood that it takes work and love to enhance that resource base. We believe you will help us make it more beautiful than it is today.

Next steps:

1. When can you arrive? As you know, yesterday is not too soon. HA!

2. We will put together a very rough draft for an agreement. Some things we probably can't iron out until you get here, and we can just sit down and create a plan together.

Please let us know that you received this email, that you do indeed accept the opportunity. We'll create a very rough understanding agreement and get back to you right away.

Again, we are very honored and excited to have you on board. Buxton will be in good hands. We hope this is the beginning of a long-term relationship that will massage another piece of earth into greater health.

Best regards,
Joel Salatin
Polyface Farm

It felt like we'd won the lottery. Farming full-time on nearly a thousand acres of land next to a national forest was a dream come true. We celebrated the news with good friends, and then we got super busy with the details of moving across the country.

A Derecho

Michael and I quickly maneuvered our way down the driveway early the next morning to check on the herd, with fence lines down they could have easily wandered up into The George Washington National Forest. We pulled up to the gate and felt immediate relief, the cows had pushed past an additional fence line and were drinking from the river. We were in luck! Allowing them access to the river wasn't usually an option, but without power we didn't have a choice. The cows were temporarily content, so we raced back to the farm and began boxing up our frozen chickens before they started to defrost. The meat birds and eggs were our only income, and we couldn't risk losing our next paycheck.

Despite the sketchy road conditions, I drove an hour to Polyface to deliver them. Trees were down on homes, cars, and stores. Gas stations were closed. The two Virginias were in a state of emergency. Polyface was also hit hard by the storm, and lost hundreds of broilers along with their pens. Apprentices and interns struggled to put pieces of the farm back together. Losing power for long periods of time was never an issue for Polyface until that storm. Polyface apprentices, secured our frozen chickens and assured me they would pass the word to the Salatins that we could use a hand at Buxton.

On my way home, I had a meltdown. I had no idea how Michal and I would repair what the storm had destroyed; the details overwhelmed me. One minute I felt humiliated about voluntarily risking our lives for the animals, and the next, I felt as fragile as a newborn. It wasn't the first time I'd felt such extreme emotions; I had certainly experienced my fair share of challenging and dramatic circumstances in the past, but what I felt on my way back to the farm was that Buxton no longer felt like home. It was a hard thing to reconcile, but it was true.

Back at Buxton our friend Don showed up to help out. His timing was impeccable. I really didn't have it in me to load more chickens and drive all the way back to Polyface. When he mentioned his homestead had a generator I was relieved. We loaded the rest of our frozen chickens and remaining eggs for him to take home. In the short time we knew Don he had become a very good friend. He and his partner Cathy, always made themselves available to us. Their friendship became a vital part of our success at Buxton Farm. We couldn't have butchered our chickens without them our second season. In addition, we shared a passion for music and growing food. We appreciated both of them.

It wasn't even 11:00 a.m. and temperatures soared. There were so many other issues that needed attention. Our first priority was to get water to all of our broilers and turkeys. When we harvested water from the river in our five-gallon buckets, Jack came out of the woods wagging his tail. I gave him a big hug. I was so glad he was still with us. Jack was my boy.

Daniel arrived later, hooked up a generator and together we retrieved the herd from down the road. Like the rest of us, the herd was hot, agitated and moved slowly back to the farmhouse. We got all the animals fed and watered, finished cleaning up the debris, and we took a short nap.

Most Virginians were unfamiliar with the term derecho until June 29th 2012 . A derecho (pronounced "deh-REY-cho") is a widespread violent windstorm that is associated with a band of rapidly moving storms. It was one of the most destructive, deadly, fast-moving severe thunderstorm complexes in North American history, resulting in twenty-two deaths, widespread damage and millions of power outages.

The storm formed in Illinois about 11 a.m., then traveled east. It reached West Virginia at about 6 p.m. and Virginia about 8 p.m. It moved across the states at approximately seventy miles per hour. The storm brought some rain, but it was the wind that proved the most damaging. In some areas wind speeds reached up to ninety miles per hour.

As a result of the sparse and scattered population, mountainous terrain, difficult conditions, and the need for crews over a large area, power restoration was very slow. With temperatures soaring days following the storm many elderly and vulnerable people suffered from heat exhaustion. The American Red Cross shipped tens of thousands of meals to West Virginia, along with large quantities of water to residents in isolated communities. Deep in the forest at Buxton Farm trees continued to tumble over the first night after the storm. I felt numb as I listened to them fall one after another. It was hard to sleep with those unnerving sounds.

Part Two

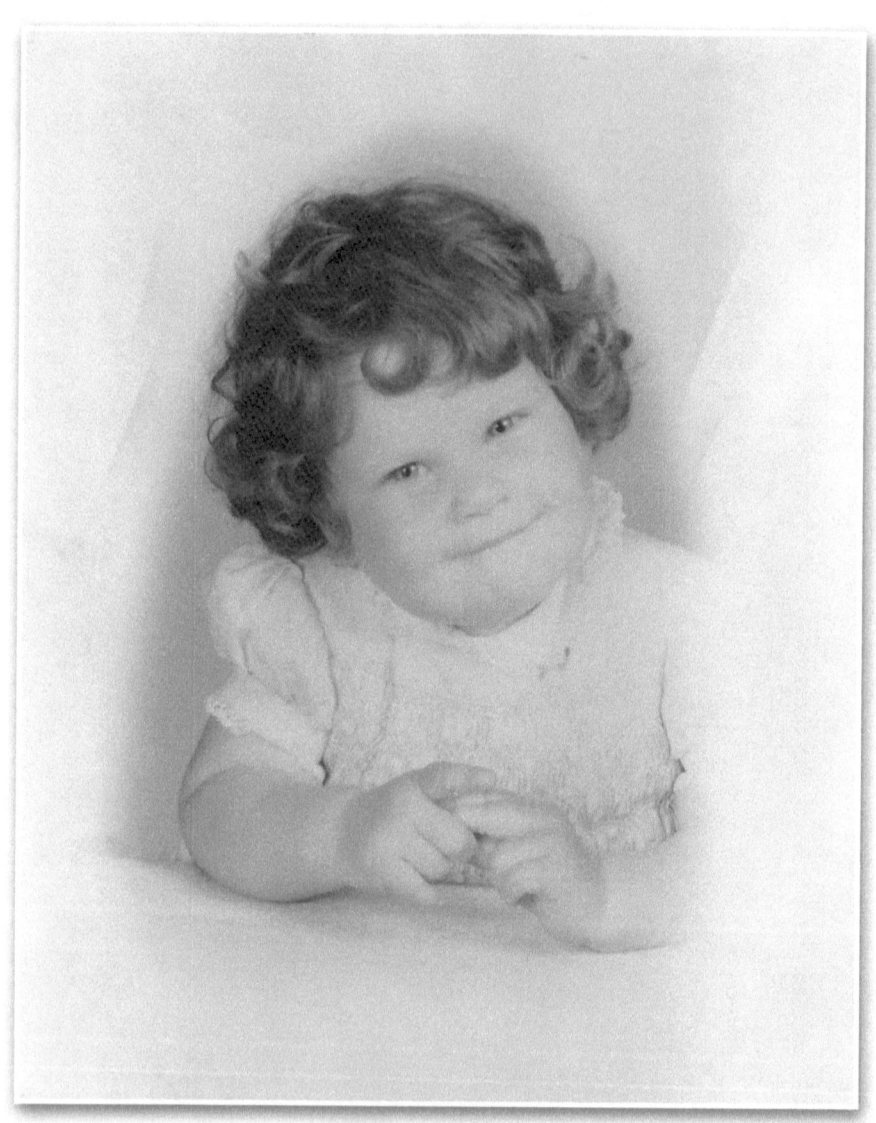

"Me at age one"

In the Beginning

For me, there was a time before. Before I felt weakened by my environment. A time when my outlook and my emotional tone for living well were intact. It was a window of time when life just felt right. In third grade, I was deeply adored. Ms. B., my teacher, probably had no idea how much her positive response filled me up, but everyday she acknowledged my strengths. In her presence, I felt sweet, funny, generous, smart, instinctual, and invincible. I adored my third grade teacher. I was loved and in love with life, as a child should be in her classroom. Her positive reflection left me feeling whole and vibrant. It was an extraordinary feeling. It left me unafraid to let my inner light shine bright in her room. I was a charismatic child, with qualities of a leader. My personality was so infectious, friends gravitated to my sense of courage. In time, I acquired a following of other like-minded adventurous students. Together, we were enthusiastic, spirited, and bold, and at lunch time we ruled the playground.

I went from a light-filled, inspiring third grade teacher to angry, repressed Catholic nuns. The bubble of love I felt from Ms. B. vanished, and although it was the same school, it was never the same for me. Without anyone to guide my intense feelings and vigorous appetite for life, I surrendered my passion for the positive. The world I once knew was deeply altered.

Every circle or organization I was involved in at Catholic school had expectations or rules of right behavior and wrong behavior. I felt pressure to fit in accordingly with each cluster of students. Being Catholic, attitudes were often harsh and extremely judgmental. At school and in church, we were told over and over we were sinners who evolved from a bad seed. I felt guilt for just being alive.

When I did something disapproving at home, I earned the silent treatment. Basically, I'd be ignored for an inordinate amount of time. I was a sensitive child. The withdrawal of attention was worse than being whipped. I took that kind of punishment hard, and felt an unyielding pressure to be a good girl. But deep inside, I didn't want to be good; I wanted to be loved.

It was unusual to know someone who had sisters old enough to be their parents. In my case I had three: Pam, Erin and Chris. There was at least twenty years between me and them. I was born when my mother, Audrey, was forty-one years old, and being the youngest, I was referred to as "the baby" of the family.

My favorite pastime was Friday night T.V. with Mom. It was a wholesome window of time together, our personal Friday night ritual. When Mom settled herself on our fake leather couch, I descended beneath her and made long trails of M&Ms across our thin plaid carpet. Sugar had a way with me even then. I popped one, two, five at a time in my mouth, while Esther Williams swam in deep water across our T.V. screen. She was beautiful and radiant, I envied her carefree nature. Some nights it was Fred Astaire and Ginger Rogers, they glided into every move with an effortless sway, I longed to move my body like them.

Mom was a woman of routine, order, and religion. She worked hard to keep a nice home. Every evening she cooked family meals. She did laundry on Mondays, cleaned the house on Tuesdays, went grocery shopping on Wednesdays, played bridge on Thursdays, and got her hair set on Fridays. You were challenged if you tried to come between her and her weekly schedule.

Her view of the world was very rigid. Dominated by Catholicism, she had strict assumptions about how people should live and behave, especially women. She intended for one of her seven daughters to join the convent and become a Catholic nun. A life of service wasn't entirely unappealing to me, but life as a nun was the last thing on my earnest and creative mind. Many times I felt guilty for my unwillingness to fulfill her wish.

Mom didn't like change or novelty, and had the same friends since grade school. She rarely felt the need to let other women in that circle. My parents kept an active social life. In fall and winter, they had bridge club, dinner dates, weekend trips, dancing, or entertaining friends at different residences. Being the social butterfly I was, I enjoyed visiting with their friends when club night was at our house.

Mom always looked forward to her short reprieve from responsibilities on Saturday nights where she got to dress up for a night on the town. My sisters and I couldn't wait to settle down in front of the T.V. as soon as they left the house. Like almost everyone else our age, weekend favorites were "Saturday Night Live" with Jane Curtin, Gilda Radner, Dan Akroyd, John Belushi and the rest of the gang from the early days of SNL. The cast members were absolutely irresistible. Their crazy antics and feral characters were the heart and soul of our weekends. It was a perfect Saturday night if we caught "The Carol Burnett Show" before SNL. We counted on those comedy shows to bring us joy.

My father worked in a job he despised and brought his problems from work home. Evening meals, we listened to him rant and rave about how crooked other people were. He was suspicious of everyone, and insisted anyone outside of our family was not to be trusted. It was the wrong ambience to hear about all the threatening things life had in store for me. Ingesting food with his anger was a lethal combination and ultimately resulted in a tug of war with food later in my life. He painted a bleak and untrustworthy world, and then insisted we pay homage to a loving creator at church on Sundays. Rarely did I feel any connection to a benevolent God in those Sunday gatherings. Instead, I discovered my relationship to a higher power when I was outdoors surrounded by mother nature.

The same routine day after day in Catholic School deadened my spirit. I craved expression, creativity, fresh air, and movement. When there was a field trip or an interruption to the monotony of our daily schedule, I was ecstatic. I could spread my wings and indulge my imagination. The potential for a positive life bubbled over inside of me, but my unconventional nature was deemed a distraction in the classroom because nuns wanted order, stability and control. The energy of an eager student like me must have felt like a threat.

Many times I was too tense to grasp what the nuns were teaching us. In fifth grade I was intimidated by Sister D., a short round nun with piercing eyes and large framed glasses. Learning Math in her class was extremely challenging for me because she was so unpredictable. I felt anxious and guarded in her presence. No matter how hard I tried pleasing Sister D., she always found something I did disapproving. Although her classroom was no place for idle thoughts, she had a large window that overlooked the cemetery adjacent to our school. In spring and fall the trees in that graveyard were not only magnificent, but they were also the perfect distraction for my curious mind.

I was envious of a friend who was a gifted artist. Every week in Sister J.'s religion class we were required to color a scene from The New Testament in our coloring book. It was a weekly competition where the winner was rewarded with a candy bar of their choice. My friend's artistic gift made it almost impossible for anyone else to win. She became one of Sister J.'s favorite students. Many times I tried winning that competition, but my earnest efforts went unrecognized. I was envious of my friend and yearned to be in her shoes, on the affectionate side of Sister J.

There was pressure from every direction to behave in a certain way. If I stepped out of line, the nuns picked me out of groups and humiliated me. I developed a reputation for being a troublemaker. Teachers were warned about me and my friends. They often separated us from one another and used punishment to scare and control us. But that only made matters worse: I rebelled. My insubordinate spirit was born in Catholic grade school.

By the time I was in eighth grade I lost respect for many of the nuns and I began acting out. Sister C.'s classroom was the perfect environment. As soon as she would turn her back to write on the chalkboard, I summoned the whole class to throw spitballs in her direction. Other times when she wasn't looking, I encouraged classmates to confuse her by switching seats. Her small frame and fragile personality made her an easy target. A few times we pushed that poor little nun to the edge until she cried.

School became a game for me. I found ways to survive the constraints and the rigidity by developing a tough exterior and acting like nothing bothered me. But inside that sensitive part of me grew more confused, angry, and disappointed.

I lived for the day softball season began. After long winters, I couldn't wait to get outside into the fresh air, move my body and feel the speed of my step. I took all my personal frustrations and put them into playing sports. I played shortstop, was quick on my feet and extremely competitive. The team counted on me to hit home runs, and I did. I was a tomboy up to bat. The rush of winning in sports and playing a good game was intoxicating. I was voted most valuable player more than once. I longed for my parents support at my athletic games, but they rarely came to see what all the fuss was about. I was embarrassed by their lack of attendance and made excuses to my friends for their absence. My self-esteem was bruised every time they didn't show. Fortunately, our devoted softball coach acknowledged my talent. His support was an essential element in building my confidence as an athlete.

My sister Amy was five years older than me and played surrogate mother at different times in my life. Closest in age to me was my other sister Kerry. The three of us were very close, and when things were challenging at home we bonded.

Dad had a routine habit of drinking hard after business meetings. It was a habit of his we grew accustomed to over time. One night crystallized the effect his binge drinking had on my sisters and me. We were in grade school and getting ready for bed when he came home drunk. As always, Mom was furious because when Dad drank too much he became a different person; one she didn't like or approve of. My sisters and I huddled together upstairs while they berated one another with harsh language. The next thing we knew, Mom left the house, and Amy, Kerry and I were left to deal with our drunken father alone. Together we sat shaking as he threatened their divorce. He convinced us he was leaving the family and that we would be lost without him. His threats terrified me. After that incident it was impossible for me to sleep, so I drank Nyquil to soothe my nerves. The alcohol in the cough medicine eliminated my fears and put me right to sleep. I knew exactly where to turn when I was overwhelmed or upset from that point forward.

"My sister Amy standing in front. My sisters Kerry and Kim on the left horse. Me with my sister Chris on the horse to the right"

Life Outdoors

My love for the natural world started at a young age and since then nature has always been a place of refuge for me. It was the only place as a child I didn't feel self-conscious. When we moved from Dayton, Ohio to Cincinnati, Ohio for my father's job, my parents chose a great spot to build our new home. There was open space and rolling hills just outside our front door. I escaped the drama of my home environment and the pressures of school by exploring in nature. Outside became my personal place of restoration. I strolled alone beside creek beds at the end of our dead-end street where it was quiet and peaceful. I felt free running through pastures with horses and cows. I climbed trees, picked apples and blackberries and rode my bike on dirt paths through the woods. Old rustic barns at the end of our road fascinated me. Friends and I made forts out of straw bales inside those old structures, and played spin the bottle with boys from our neighborhood. My first kiss took place inside one of those forts, along with the beginning of my first crush. I nursed that crush for years. I still remember his name. Those private outdoor places nurtured my spirit in subtle ways.

My brother Brian was the middle sibling and the only boy in our family. In winter at Thondore's pond he made a bonfire for us to gather around and sip hot chocolate. Bitter cold temperatures didn't faze either of us. Brian played ice hockey, and my sisters and I skated with friends from our neighborhood. I zipped across that solid ice without a care in the world. I was in my element moving my body in the crisp, frigid air. I loved being out in nature any time of the year.

When my sister Erin moved to Florida Mom and Dad decided as a family we would travel there for Christmas. Seven of us squeezed into Dad's brand new Chevrolet. It was an eighteen hour drive. "Bye Bye Miss American Pie," by Don McClean was the most popular song that year. It was one of my favorite songs and the radio played it over and over. In order to pass time, the whole family sang along. The song lifted our spirits and made the time pass. To this day I can't hear that song without thinking about that family excursion.

Summers were filled with easy entertainment. Evenings we caught fireflies, played kick the can and ghost in the graveyard, grilled out, shared late night swims, and camped out under the stars. Some of the best memories with my family took place outside in summer. There was always an unspoken permission to breathe deeper in summer or spring, as if life outdoors lifted our spirits. Several of our vacations were spent at Hilton Head in South Carolina. It was a great place for my parents to play golf, their favorite sport. Although golf never interested me, I tagged along just so I could drive the golf cart recklessly throughout the course. It was a favorite pastime of mine that drove my parents crazy.

I was fourteen years old when I became an Aunt for the first time. My new nephew was adorable with a head full of red curly locks, and chubby cheeks. He was the highlight of our vacation that summer. When my sister Chris and her family joined us on our summer getaways our family always felt more complete. On those family reprieves from daily life, we forgot about our problems, differences, and struggles. We swam in the ocean, ate picnics on the beach, and played games or cards late into the night. I appreciated my family for turning me on to the ocean at a young age. I knew I would follow water from that point forward in my life.

I was too young to remember my oldest sister Pam's first two husbands. But Gil, her third husband, was a very successful businessman who adored my sister. He owned and managed Gilbert Sporting Goods Company, and after they were married they ran his business as a team. It was a very lucrative business, and as a result Pam and Gil were very generous with the rest of the family. Some of the trips we took were a direct result of Pam's desire to treat us to new places.

My sister lived in beautiful homes and drove fancy cars. On Sundays she would visit and take the family for a cruise in her Rolls Royce. Other times she arrived in their two-seater Mercedes Benz Sports edition, my favorite. Her life was filled with exotic trips, beautiful clothes, fancy restaurants, and second homes. Her expensive taste was something I admired. With no children of her own, she enjoyed sharing her opulent lifestyle with her younger siblings.

Mom was a stay-at-home parent, and Dad's income as a food salesman was meager. Money was always an issue with my parents, but after Pam married Gil, our lifestyle was upgraded. I felt torn between money being a positive thing and feeling bought with the material gifts. It wasn't until later in my life that I realized how my sister's abundant lifestyle affected me in positive ways. Eventually I understood that money doesn't buy happiness, but in many ways it can make life easier.

Pam and Gil owned a farm tucked away in a quiet part of the countryside in Ohio. Spending weekends there was an experience I always looked forward to. Together we rode her horses across the countryside. The pleasure that farm gave me was undeniable. Thanks to Pam and my other sisters, I was entrusted with a deep regard for animals at a very young age. When I was three years old, my older sisters put me on one of their horses, and without realizing it someone turned away and I slipped right off that horse onto the ground. My right arm broke. After that injury healed, I was right back up on that horse. Fear or no fear, I was going to know the thrill of riding horses with my big sisters.

What's Wrong With Me?

I was barely fourteen years old when I started drinking alcohol. On weekends friends and I waited outside our local convenience store asking strangers to buy us beer. If we were unsuccessful finding the right candidate to make the purchase, we found another way; there was always a way. It didn't really matter what kind of beer it was; we drank to feel liberated. The first time I drank champagne, I didn't want to stop. The smooth fizzy drink went down my throat without any effort. Like beer, it made my insides warm.

One evening before our school's summer festival, my friends and I drank several bottles of cheap champagne, loaded our purses with a few cold beers, and set out for a good time. It didn't take much for me to feel the untroubled world of inebriation. I welcomed it. Once the champagne kicked in, I felt light as a feather. I floated across the parking lot into our school festival with a grin as wide as Texas. I guzzled a beer and as soon as it was finished, I threw the empty bottle over my shoulder, where it went crashing to the ground. Everyone turned to see what the ruckus was. My friends feared suspension from school so they pulled me aside and scolded me for being so careless. I was totally unaware of any personal consequences and oblivious to their concerns. Alcohol restored my invincibility; it became an elixir of choice.

I imagined high school would bring me freedom. My first year was exciting, interesting, challenging and rewarding. I made new friends, gained confidence and I was thrilled to be in a different environment. I engaged in social activities like cheerleading, journalism, photography, and student council. I loved Friday night football games and the physical expression that came with cheerleading. The crowd, the lights, the camaraderie, the boys. For a while I participated in these events with all my heart.

My parents expected me to assist with part of my Catholic high school tuition, so my second year in high school I got my first job at a fast food restaurant. I don't remember how I chose it, but working at Kentucky Fried Chicken helped pay for my education. I worked as a cashier, but my job responsibilities also included making biscuits, cleaning, and supervising the front of the restaurant. Making the biscuits was my favorite part of that job because I could eat as many as I wanted. At the end of each shift, my body was covered in grease, and my uniform and hair reeked of fried chicken. My parents made it clear to me that if I decided to go to college, I was totally responsible for paying my own way, so I kept that part-time job all through high school. Most of my friends didn't have those kinds of responsibilities. I envied them for having parents that supported them financially. With my tough exterior, I played the disappointment down as if it wasn't a big deal, but in weaker moments, I interpreted the lack of financial assistance as a lack of love.

I grew up with siblings who embraced the hippie culture. My sister Kim was the fourth daughter and the first person I knew who did LSD. I was barely four years old when Dad had to coax her down out of a tree during a bad trip. My brother Brian was the first person who influenced my decision to smoke marijuana. I noticed his personality changed after he got high with friends, suddenly everything was funny and lighthearted. The shift in their attitudes from serious to easygoing made me very curious.

Brian was very popular in public school, and during dinner we were constantly interrupted with people calling for him. In those days answering machines and voicemail were nonexistent, so our home telephone rang off the hook for him. He was definitely the kind of guy who was easy to like, but no one had that many friends. When my parents learned he was growing and selling marijuana, they threatened to kick him out of the house. Marijuana was easy to get even back then, and freely offered at parties after Friday night football games. I'm not sure exactly the first time I got high, but in the beginning it soothed me. Taking a few hits off of a joint was nothing like smoking cigarettes. Not only did marijuana taste better, it also smelled amazing. There was something ritualistic or tribal about sharing a joint with friends. In the early days smoking weed to take the edge off felt like a promising solution to my worries and my lack of self-confidence. Once I was high, I was less self conscious, more easygoing and prone to laughter. I quickly understood why so many people felt getting high improved the quality of their lives. But the longer I continued smoking pot I increased my intake. What started off as a carefree harmless experience, turned into an unpleasant addiction that left me feeling paranoid and alone.

By the time I was a junior in high school, all passion I had for school was gone. I was bored with my classes and I couldn't relate to my studies, my friends, or the activities that brought me joy my first two years of high school. Without understanding how to express my need to be an individual, I went to great extremes to be part of the peanut gallery, even though I rarely felt I had nothing in common with them. I showed up for classes and events but inside I felt vacant. At the heart of my distress was the imminent feeling that something was wrong with me.

My father sold food for a living to grocery stores, and some of his accounts included Sara Lee, Kellogg's, Green Giant, Mrs. Paul's, as well as candy accounts. Incidentally, whenever I needed extra cash I would knock on neighbors doors and sell Dad's frozen foods to them at discounted prices. I'm not sure if neighbors bought groceries from me because they actually needed them, or if they just couldn't say no to me. Either way, my entrepreneurial spirit for selling food was born hustling frozen foods.

In those days, he brought home unprecedented amounts of Tootsie Rolls, Clark Bars, Tootsie Pops and other sweets. Because I lived with my very own sugar daddy, I developed a habit of turning to his confectionary stash to relieve overwhelming feelings of doubt and depression.

In the beginning it was a little here and a little there, but then, like alcohol and marijuana, food became another way to suppress my feelings and avoid my unhappy world. If no one was home after school, I had a field day in the kitchen. I devoured peanut butter and jelly on saltines, bowls of Captain Crunch and Cocoa Krispies, toasted white bread with butter and sugar, Oreo cookies, candy bars, Sara Lee cakes, and ice cream. Whatever junk food we had in the house, I found it. After binging I would lie down, bloated, then fall asleep until dinner. My sisters would decide on having a homemade chocolate chip cookie for dessert, only to discover I ate all of them. I was so out of control with my binging that my family had to hide food from me. Even though I hated what I was doing to my body, I had no clues on how to stop the viscous cycle. I lived in the shadow of addiction where everything felt meaningless. The crazy thing about an addict is that in the beginning, my intentions always started out pure. I'd go to parties and promise myself one of this or one of that, and when I followed through, I was proud of my self-discipline. But those insights were rare. Too many occasions, I abandoned personal convictions at the door. By the end of the night I was stoned, intoxicated or bloated. I hardly recognized the person I was becoming.

I became friends with a guy a few years older than me. When we first met, I was drawn to him because he was fearless. That should have been a strong indicator to me that he was also insane, but being teenagers, I was too young to see that as a sign; I was looking for love in all the wrong places. He came from an affluent lifestyle, and so we enjoyed water skiing, boating trips, fancy cars, and impressive parties at his house. Like my siblings, his older brother was a big influence in his life, and we wanted to be like them, so together, we grew up fast.

In summer, I would sneak out of my house in the middle of the night with a girlfriend, and meet up with him and his friends. Long before any of us had our licenses, we cruised around in his parents van drinking beer and listening to Led Zeppelin. For a while I was seduced by his wild side. He seemed invincible and lived on the edge. But then I realized I was too young to settle for just one guy. Once he knew I wanted my freedom, his possessive nature became a nightmare. I couldn't get away from him. I wanted out of that relationship as much as I wanted a way out of binging and using, but I felt powerless to do either. He became physically abusive and hit me one night in my family's home. My sister Amy heard us arguing and intervened. The following day, I went to the doctor because the assault blocked the hearing of my right ear, and my face was black and blue. Embarrassed about my condition, I lied and told the doctor I fell off my bike. That incident should have been an awakening for my parents to protect me from his unpredictable behavior, but he was very clever and he immediately found a way back into my life. Even though the physical abuse didn't continue, I didn't summon the courage to get away from him for a few more years. I was sorry it took so long.

High school was supposed to be fun, but for me it was nothing but effort and unkept promises. Being deep into an eating disorder, partying, and in a suffocating relationship, my grades slipped and my ability to focus collapsed. I started to isolate from friends and fell deeper into depression. Lunchtime was typically a social network gathering, but unable to put a happy face on for anyone, I started eating alone or not eating in school at all.

I knew how to act in order to fit in with specific cliques, but as high school continued, I really didn't want to belong with any of them. In fact, I wanted out of the whole paradigm. Whenever my father drove me to class on his way to work, he tried to convince me high school should be some of the best years of my life. I remember thinking, if it doesn't get any better than this, then what's the point? Life felt so meaningless. I tried to like school and be happy, but it was useless. Inside those walls felt like a prison.

I sought support from a counselor at school. She encouraged me to be more positive, but it was like putting a bandage over an open wound. I was raw and had no resources for handling my feelings. I sensed she wasn't someone who could help me get to the heart of my problems, so our sessions were short-lived.

Desperate for help with my eating disorder, I tried Overeaters Anonymous in order to stop binging. In OA I had to journal about the foods I ate, call my sponsor, or get to a meeting if I felt a binge coming on. Sometimes I had to weigh my food. Those meetings were helpful because finally, I was in a room where people were talking about their emotions and feelings. No one else in my life was. Instead, they moved through life exclaiming, "No pain, no gain." In those meetings, I started to see how I was at the mercy of my emotions. They were running my life. I was the youngest person in those OA meetings, and I got teased at home about them. I second-guessed my need to get help and ultimately quit going. Deep inside, I knew that was a decision I'd live to regret.

My sister Amy took me to a food doctor who gave overweight people shots in the rear end in order to help curb their appetites. A few friends had results with the shots and claimed they took away cravings. The doctor was a strange tiny woman who seemed to enjoy needling girls' butts. The shots hurt and were expensive.It was dangerous territory to believe a shot in the ass could clean up my life and take away my troubles. This was long before prescription drugs were handed out to young people like vitamins. We weren't given psychological labels yet, like manic-depressive or bipolar.

Against the Wind

Dark hair, dark eyes, and a deep regard for life, my sister Amy, was a creative woman who showed me I could do anything I put my mind to as long as I was passionate about it. She had incredible discipline and became a successful business woman as a result of her unfettered intentions.

We grew up in middle-class Catholic white suburbia where diversity was nonexistent. It was the 70's and from what I observed, people were still uneasy around anyone who wasn't white. Our only connection to African-Americans was after Sunday Mass when Dad drove through Over The Rhine, the poorest part of downtown Cincinnati. I'm not sure what we were supposed to gain from observing poor black people struggling to survive, but it was an uncomfortable environment to witness. On our drive back to middle class white suburbia I was overcome with feelings of guilt.

One summer day after a long day canoeing and drinking on the Little Miami River with friends, I returned home hung over and discovered a black man in our kitchen. I knew Amy's date was coming over to cook dinner for her, but she didn't tell anyone that Blair, her new boyfriend wasn't white. Without hesitation my parents left the house. Mom was insulted and threatened not to come back until Blair was gone. My parents came from a generation of prejudiced thinkers and tried influencing us with the same limited thoughts. I didn't see what the big deal was so I went up to my room and passed out.

Amy and Blair had no intention of apologizing for their relationship. They carried on as if nothing was wrong. My sister was the kind of woman who thought nothing of doing her own thing even it it meant going against the wind. Later on, we came to understand they had been dating for some time. Amy confided in me that she was in love with Blair.

For the next four years there was constant bickering between Amy and our parents. The arguments were tedious and annoying. She was scolded for "shacking up" with a black man. My parents exclaimed over and over the relationship would never work. I think it would have been easier for my sister if she had just moved out into her own place and did her own thing, but she stayed strong and didn't let my parents' opinions influence her love for Blair. I don't think our parents initially realized how stubborn and strong-willed their children could be at times. The arguments got old, and in time Blair grew on them. Before we knew it, he became part of our family. Blair was funny, creative, smart, artistic and entertaining. He brought the gift of laughter into all of our lives and was a great addition to our dramatic family. I was thrilled to be in their wedding. Amy insisted they get married in our Catholic parish. I don't think a mixed race wedding had ever happened in white suburbia until Amy and Blair. She had exceptional integrity. At the reception, Blair had everyone on the dance floor. He performed with the band and sang love ballads to his new wife. We all were certain their challenges were behind them and their futures together were bright.

Together, Amy and Blair opened up Aunt Maudie's Comedy Club in Over the Rhine, Cincinnati. Amy hired me as a cocktail waitress and my boyfriend as bartender. It was a funky comedy club that attracted all kinds of interesting talent. My sister ran that club with detailed precision. My family shared a lot of good times at that club. It stayed open for a few years before Blair's career as a comedian and entertainer took him on the road full-time.

University Life and Sobriety

I took the usual steps of applying for colleges, but without any specific direction about my future or what I wanted to study, I had no idea where I belonged, so I chose a college where I'd spent weekends partying in high school. The university I enrolled in was far from anything that represented me. I was totally uncomfortable and out of my league in an academically inclined environment. In truth, I didn't belong in college at all but no one could have told me that. I had to find out for myself.

My first roommate was part African-American and Korean. She had a brilliant mind and an incredible appetite for getting stoned. She dabbled in all kinds of different drugs and people flocked to our room to be entertained by her. She was exotic, unafraid of living on the edge, and she made a career out of shocking people with her body, behavior, and beliefs. Her life experience and habits were way too progressive for the Catholic girl in me. In order for me to survive my first year at the university, I had to get a new roommate. Eventually I moved down the hall from her. We remained friends, but she wasn't someone I could bring home from college for a weekend; my parents would have had me committed.

College became a waste of precious time and money. I made many promises to myself to get my act together my first year, but I didn't keep any of them. Not only was my eating disorder in full bloom but I was also abusing alcohol and drugs on a regular basis. Between food binging and sampling new drugs, I had little time to study.

Music has always been a positive influence in my life. When the band, "The Talking Heads" came to our campus for a live concert, friends and I waited weeks in anticipation to see them live. Unfortunately, the night of the concert I smoked an exorbitant amount of pot. Too much pot. By the time the concert started I was too high to enjoy the evening so I went home and passed out. I had looked forward to that concert with great enthusiasm. The following day I was disgusted with myself for missing it. My addictive personality was starting to get under my skin. After that incident I started to desire a different kind of life, primarily one with meaning.

I thought religion was the answer to my problems so I joined a group of born again Christians on our campus. I embraced the feeling of elation and worship in those weekly gatherings. I also enjoyed a short brief reprieve from alcohol and drugs. I tried convincing friends to join me in my bible study group but they insisted I was being brainwashed. They even accused me of being part of a cult. For awhile their opinions fell on deaf ears but over time their influences were too convincing for me to resist. Eventually they won me over. I picked up partying right where I left off. By this time a lot of my friends were into dropping acid. As much as I enjoyed a good time, taking acid was something that never appealed to me. Ever since my sister Kim had a bad trip, I was terrified of trying it so I steered clear of it. It was a decision I never regretted.

At the end of my first year, the coed dorm I lived in had its annual spring bash. I was drawn to a blond-haired, blue-eyed guy with a great smile. He was visiting his best friend who lived downstairs. We were introduced that weekend and had our first date. He was super smart with a very sharp mind, and an intensity about him that fascinated me. I was thrilled to spend time with someone who seemed original. Our relationship was filled with novelty and adventure. I spent that summer break working as a camp counselor and on my days off my new boyfriend visited. We took walks in the countryside and road horses together. When camp was over I temporarily moved home and I introduced him to my family. He became part of our weekly gatherings. After a few weeks of dating I joined his family for dinner and a few family events. My new relationship was lighthearted and distinctive. Love was in the air.

We dated six months when his mother committed suicide. The night she took her life we had declined a request to join his parents for dinner.

Even though I didn't know her intimately yet, guilt plagued both us for ignoring their invitation. I was in my second year of college and questioning what I was doing back at the university. I'm not sure what I thought I could do, but after his mom committed suicide I dropped out of college, and I took it upon myself to try and rescue him from his grief. I was good friends with my new roommate and she was disappointed and shocked when I told her I was leaving school and moving home. My two sisters, Amy and Kerry, drove to the university and helped me pack my belongings. As soon as we drove off that campus, I felt a tremendous amount of relief.

Eager to help my boyfriend recover from his loss, I devoted all of my time and energy to him. But heartache shattered the sweet guy I once knew and adored. Instead of seeking counseling, he got deeper into drugs and became belligerent. His rage was too much for me to bear, so our relationship ended.

As it happens, meeting him was the best thing that happened to me in college. At the time it appeared I left school to help him, but in the end, the transition worked in my favor. I moved home, enrolled in a small college, bought a car, got a job, and I got sober. Boyfriend or no boyfriend, it was time to get my act together. Living with a host of unfulfilled desires finally caught up to me. I joined Alcoholics Anonymous and found a whole new world waiting for me.

At first, living sober was very strange for me. Waking up clear-minded was akin to living in a foreign country. I was shaky and uncertain I could really live without using or binging. It was a day by day painstaking process. In order to distract myself from any temptations, I went to ninety AA meetings in ninety days, started smoking cigarettes to calm my nerves, and even though I didn't like coffee, I drank it at meetings. I was no longer comfortable in bars or at parties where drinking was the main focus. I made new friends in AA and got my first sponsor. She emphasized the twelve steps which were based on admitting a number of things. First, I was powerless over alcohol and my life had become unmanageable. Next, I had to turn my life over to a higher power of my choice, examine my past, and make amends to people I had hurt. Once the steps were integrated into my daily life, then I had to share the message of recovery and be of service to other people. In addition to working the steps, I also started a daily journal. Day by day the fog lifted.

The smaller college worked out great for me because the classes were more intimate. I was less intimidated with fewer students and looked forward to my studies. I rented an apartment from a college professor, worked two jobs, and dated a guy who was also sober. He also introduced me to intellectually stimulating things, which I really appreciated. His sense of humor and his wittiness about life were refreshing. He introduced me to Victor Frankl's book, *Man's Search for Meaning*. Frankl's courage and commitment to be optimistic in spite of dire circumstances as an Auschwitz Concentration Camp Inmate during World War II astonished me. Somehow I related to his powerful message and story. Although my reality was no comparison to the dire conditions of living and working in a Nazi concentration camp, my impending desire to know the true purpose of life was irrefutable. If Frankl could find something positive to focus on as an inmate surrounded by death and suffering, there was no reason why I couldn't overcome my feelings of despair and depression. Frankl became one of my personal heroes.

My sober boyfriend and I discovered a whole new world together. He was studying to be an artist and his teacher needed nude models for their drawing class. I wondered if modeling nude in a safe environment would help me feel better about my body. The idea intrigued me, so I applied. It was a big leap for this Catholic gal. Even though I was eager to push my boundaries in a new context, in the end it was too extreme for my taste. I'm not sure what it did for me, except prove to myself that I could do frightening things sober.

I finished college with a B.A. in Elementary Education and taught inner-city school. I substituted for the public school system, and enjoyed not being tied down to one grade or one specific location. I floated. Some days I would substitute teach in the inner city and other days the suburbs. Every day was different, and the variety was perfect for me. I loved working with the kids, and in a way, I hoped to become the kind of teacher Ms. B. was for me in third grade.

After teaching in Ohio for a year, my older sister Erin encouraged me to move to California. She called from Los Angeles weekly and described the magnificent sunsets on the beach where she rode her bike every evening after work. I imagined the water, warmth, and carefree people and was green with envy.

The last time I'd visited California was when I was a freshman in college. I flew out West and met up with two guy friends from my dorm. We stayed with my sister for about ten days and got stoned every day. Venice Beach, Hollywood, Mexico, San Diego, Santa Monica. Erin gave us a tour of all her favorite spots, and we partied up and down the coast. In Ensenada, Mexico, we partied in an old dive bar that tourists frequented for the tequila and the ambience. Inside that old bar it was like the Wild West. We let go of all our inhibitions. One tequila shot after another, we toasted to life with complete strangers. Very few people left that bar walking. Not one of us was capable of driving that night, but one of the guys took the wheel. Trying to find our way home, we almost drove straight off a cliff into the sea. It was a miracle we made it home. In the middle of the night, the buzz wore off and the hangover kicked in. I felt like I had been punched in the stomach with a sack of poison. Inside our sweet beach bungalow, I hugged the toilet, desperate for relief. The next day I could hardly function; my hangover was relentless.

Just thinking about that trip to California made me shudder. But I was sober a few years now and my desire for something new was undeniable. My sister planted the seed for me to move out West and her timing was perfect. At that time we were inundated with two weeks of nonstop rain and no sunshine. Ohio was dark, cold and bitter. It was pure dread. I could barely get out of bed in the morning to get to my teaching job. The cold weather and lack of sunshine weakened my spirit. In truth, I was ready for a change. The good news was my sister Kerry lived down south near Laguna Niguel with her husband, and Erin lived in Santa Monica. With AA as my support group and two sisters nearby, I felt confident about the move. Fortunately, I had postponed signing a teaching contract with the public schools. I could teach anywhere. I was free!

In the fall of 1990, with sunny days summoning me, I packed my Toyota and drove West. My boyfriend accompanied me and we shared the driving. We didn't explore any other states. I had one destination in mind. We drove. I was determined to get to the West Coast as soon as possible.

"Me Sky Diving 1993"

City of Angels

I Immediately fell in love with the southern California climate. Having access to both the mountains and the ocean was a remarkable combination. The consistent sunshine along with living at the edge of the sea inspired me. There are many compelling reasons for living in Los Angeles, but what I immediately appreciated besides the weather was the diversity of people and the arts. I was introduced to creative, open minded, talented, and interesting people. Worldly people. Strong successful women. Women who transformed their personal stories and lived from a deep place of knowing who they are. Self-actualized women. Pioneers.

I wanted that. I wanted to live from my center. I wanted to feel confident. I wanted a rich inner life. I felt capable of so much more than I knew in Ohio. I enjoyed teaching, but I wanted more. I had ideas of traveling, exploring nature, meeting a host of different people from all over the world. I was young, curious, eager, and terribly naive. I could feel the longing I'd carried since childhood had the potential to be fulfilled out West. I was ready to broaden my understanding of life and meet people I could relate to from all walks of life. In California, I felt the promise of a better future. The West Coast became my canvas.

My Midwest upbringing was obvious to everyone I initially met. My face and body were very round. Before moving to California I waged war on my body with binging and tried hiding under frumpy clothes. I didn't have any sense of what my body was really for, until I moved out West. I had no connection to being a woman. Even in my drinking days, my body was off limits. I was a foreigner in my own skin. I had zero sense of beauty, style, and design. My hair was very thick and wavy. As a kid, Mom insisted I keep it super short like a boy. I never wavered from that style until I moved to California. Then, I let my hair grow long, and then longer, until I discovered I had a gorgeous head of hair. In California, I was free to let it flow!

The contrast between the Midwest and California was substantial. On the coast, I was surrounded by people unafraid of their bodies. People who respected and enjoyed their bodies. Some even treated them like temples to be revered and honored. I was totally unfamiliar with people comfortable in their skin, and amazed at the confidence they carried within themselves. It seemed like everyone I met was unafraid of their sexuality. Around them, I felt prudish and inexperienced. Even though I wasn't your typical well-behaved teenager, once I got to the West Coast, I felt repressed as if I had been living under a rock.

I studied to be a teacher in college because I wanted to positively influence young people, but when I moved to California, I realized what I had to give students was sketchy so I dismissed a career in teaching and immersed myself in the healing arts. I dove right into New Age philosophies. I studied breath, movement, massage, energy alignment, acupressure and aromatherapy. I gravitated toward people who knew the wisdom of integrating body, mind and spirit. I spent time studying with mentors and masters who introduced me to the chakras, the light body, metaphysics and meditation. I also studied acting, writing, dancing and the performing arts.

I got a job waiting tables in a beautiful Italian restaurant on Ocean Avenue. There was an outdoor patio that provided excellent views of the water and sunsets. I was stimulated by that view every time I worked and I made more money waiting tables than I would have teaching school full time. Plus, I had plenty of time to explore beautiful California.

Everyone on the West Coast, including myself, seemed to be looking for something. Whether it was stardom, wealth, spiritual experiences, finding one's soul mate, or expanding one's consciousness it didn't seem to matter. We were all seeking and expectant of something great.

I went skydiving, hiking, rafting, and scuba diving. I hiked, biked, and traveled all over California. It was a deeply creative, fulfilling time. Even though I enjoyed all the physical stimulation, there was also something happening deep within. I began to develop an understanding of living from the inside out.

Not only did I have a twelve-step program, I also found a therapist to guide me towards self-empowerment. The combination of metaphysical studies, therapy, and AA helped me better understand my body, my story, and where I needed healing. I carried the problems of the world on my shoulders, like the rest of my family. It was a heavy burden that clouded my psyche. Once I moved across the country, away from my roots, I realized I owed it to myself to change this story. Personal empowerment became my intention.

There was one particular AA meeting in Santa Monica that I frequented. A beautiful woman shared her story at a noon meeting one day. At the time, I was looking for a sponsor, and as she spoke I gravitated to her energy. She was healthy, healed, and happy, and I wanted what she had! At the end of the meeting, I went up to her and introduced myself, and then kindly asked her if she would sponsor me. She was very apologetic and said she traveled often and her schedule made her somewhat impossible to count on. I thanked her for sharing her experience, strength, and hope, and we parted ways. Walking out to the car, my friend Laura informed me the woman was a famous movie star. If I had known who she was, I never would have approached her. I was a newcomer to Los Angeles and embarrassed at my naiveté. It hadn't occurred to me yet that I was surrounded by the entertainment industry. It took a little time for me to get up to speed with the ground rules.

Much of what I lived those early years in the City of Angels was magical. Life-long questions were being answered, and desires fulfilled. My inner life blossomed. Living on the West Coast was a new beginning for me. Eventually I felt freer living in California. No more gloomy grey winters or unbearable rainy Mondays. This Midwestern gal was being transformed. I'm certain the City of Angels saved my life. I came alive.

Me and my six sisters at our family home in 1984.
(In front L-R) Pam, Chris, Amy, Kerry, me, Kim, and Erin

My Sister, The Hippie

Less than three months after I moved to California in 1990, my sister Kim was killed in a car accident. The news of her death was unfathomable. I flew home immediately with my sister Kerry, who was living in Laguna Niguel, California. On the rough ride back to the Midwest, we hardly spoke. Thoughts of how Kim's life ended repeated over and over in my mind. I hoped her last breath wasn't painful. It was so hard for me to accept we would never ride horses together again. I wondered what would happen to her farm, and all the animals she loved so much. I was only a year old the first time she carried me up with her to sit on one of her horses, it was a majestical feeling. One I never forgot.

Kim was the middle sibling, and closer in age to Brian our brother. She was a very passionate, intense, private woman with an affinity for horses, dogs, nature and good music. I always looked forward to family gatherings on her farm, where weekends were spent exploring the woods together on horseback. Fall was our favorite horseback riding season.

Being the baby of the family, I was enthralled by my older sister's habits. Before Kim went out on dates, I sat watching our sister Amy iron Kim's long frizzy hair. I was enamored by her eccentric habits, and too young to know she was truly the family hippie. Kim wasn't easily swayed by anyone's idea of how life should be lived. Her independence and innate self-confidence challenged our parents more than once, and as soon as she was old enough, she left home and the Catholic church in search of her true self.

When my six sisters and I got together, our loud guffaws could take over a room. Our brother Brian was always outnumbered by us. I'm not sure who we inherited such a raucous laugh from, but it's a prominent part of each one of us. I can testify that Kim's laugh was definitely the loudest. At discos or bars, she never missed an opportunity to hit the floor dancing when "I Feel Good" by James Brown played. A big fan of funk, it was one of her favorite songs. Naturally, the rest of us joined her on the dance floor. It was hard for me to accept these good times were over.

Her husband Wayne was a remarkable, kind, loving person and another welcomed addition to our dramatic Catholic family. They were on their way to look at a farmhouse for sale, when a car from the opposite side of the road hit a deer. The deer went airborne through the windshield and landed on Kim. Her neck broke instantly. Miraculously, her dog and her husband were untouched by the impact, but forever changed.

When we arrived home for her funeral, the local news station reported the accident. It was unsettling to listen to them give detailed descriptions about my sister's death on television. As a result, I never went to the accident site and wouldn't know where to place a marker where she lost her life. Instead, I tried to make peace with her untimely death on my own terms. There were so many reasons why I loved my big sister Kim, and when she died, I felt a piece of me go with her. After we buried her, I grew even more determined to redefine and claim my life. My sister was thirty five years old when she died.

I was disoriented when I returned to California after my sister's tragic death. My first night home, my friend Laura took me to an AA meeting in Malibu. In the car, while friends talked about the exciting things happening in their lives, I sat numb in the backseat. The pungent smell of the ocean and the piercing lights from the Pacific Coast Highway rattled my mind. I felt like a lump of flesh casting my heartache out to the sea the further north we drove. I was there physically, but my thoughts were far off in the distance. It was the right thing to be around people my first night back in California, but it was impossible for me to be present because my heart was back in Ohio. The time it took to heal from Kim's abrupt death was unforeseen by me. Until we buried my hippie sister, I had no idea grief could be so deep and wide.

Wounded Healer and Eternal Love

My Aunt Jo was a psychotherapist in Cleveland and into different modalities of healing. Our friendship began with a mutual respect for AA meetings and recovery and then grew into an intimate friendship with a wide range of shared interests. Aunt Jo was always reinventing herself. After a career in acting and broadcasting, she studied to be a psychotherapist at forty-six years old. She was sober a long time and spent a lot of time working with people in recovery. She was hardly five feet tall but a real powerhouse.

She visited me my first Christmas in California and since she was friends with Jane Buffett, we ended up housesitting for Jimmy Buffett's family at their Malibu home. It was a sweet home on the Pacific Coast Highway overlooking the ocean. For two weeks Jo and I enjoyed glorious sunsets, early morning swims, and nighttime hot-tubbing.

We both shared a desire to know more about the body's ability to heal itself. On one of her visits to California we drove to The Healing Light Center in Pasadena to attend a class with the founder and Medicine woman: Rosalyn Bruyere. Her book, *"Wheels of Light, A Study of the Chakras,"* was one of my first introductions to light energy and hands-on healing. Through Rosalyn's work I also discovered Emilie Conrad's work in Continuum. Rosalyn and Emilie participated in a research experiment at UCLA with Dr. Valerie Hunt, in which the existence and significance of the human aura was proven and measured scientifically. Their groundbreaking work was new to me but on the leading edge, exactly where I wanted to be!

I took classes with Rosalyn for a few years and volunteered at her center. Eventually I received weekly "hands on healing" sessions with a healer trained by Rosalyn. The sessions were unlike anything I had ever come across back in Ohio. I was introduced to my body's innate sense of intelligence and wisdom. Once I comprehended the significance of the chakra's (a Sanskrit term for energy points in the body), I felt an incredible amount of personal potential replace years of repression and fear. The sessions played an integral part of reconnecting me to my body and taught me important techniques that served me in my next career as a massage therapist.

From The Healing Light Center I moved on to study massage at the Institute of Psycho-Structural Balancing. When I moved across the country I never intended to start a career touching people, but as I probed deeper into my own healing, I felt the healing power of touch so naturally I became inspired to alleviate stress and pain in other people through professional massage.

At first, I was a little taken back by the intimacy required in massage. There is a certain level of vulnerability that comes with giving a stranger permission to touch you. It took a few professional sessions until I was hooked. I became so enthralled with the therapeutic effects of massage that I couldn't help but wonder if more people were introduced to it at a younger age, then maybe as a culture, we would have a baseline of respect and appreciation for our bodies. Instead of feeling inhibited and disconnected from my body I began to develop a feeling of reverence for it. Massage was a gateway into other modalities of healing. Studying and giving massage became another source of personal empowerment and fulfillment.

My first job as a massage therapist was in the Spa at The Peninsula Hotel in Beverly Hills. It was a beautiful hotel with a very distinguished clientele and the perfect place for me to start a part-time career as a bodyworker. A lot of the clients I worked on regularly were directors, producers, actors, and relatives of famous actors. Some of them were very demanding, but that only made me want to be a better massage therapist. After the Peninsula Hotel I built up a small but significant private practice in an office nearby.

I massaged a lot of women who went under the knife to improve their looks, some of them more than once. Face lifts, implants, Botox, tummy tucks, upper arm tucks, you name it. Once women got started with plastic surgery, they usually didn't stop. Being surrounded by the entertainment industry, people put great emphasis on looking good. It took conscious effort not to get sucked into the superficial side of Los Angeles.

I had the privilege of going to Marlon Brando's house once to give a massage to one of his relatives whom I worked on for a couple of years. As I drove across Mulholland Drive to get to his home, I could see why famous people secluded themselves in those mountains; the views of Los Angeles were stunning. After being let into his private gate, I pulled up the driveway to the house where there were huge signs with large print that read: DO NOT GET OUT OF YOUR CAR. HONK YOUR HORN. Within seconds, several enormous dogs surrounded my car. I can't recall what kind of dogs they were, but they were large beasts and reminded me of lions. It was unnerving. Finally, someone came out to walk me inside. I was careful not to make a fast move. The dogs seemed friendly but were very good at their job, I was terribly intimidated by all of them. Providing massage for one of Marlon Brando's relatives wasn't unusual for me, but being invited to his estate to work was a rare occasion. I knew a lot of people who would have appreciated being in my shoes that day.

My life has been inspired by charismatic people. People with vision. The desire to surround myself with passionate teachers has shaped my world and put me in extraordinary circumstances. The first conversation I had with Emilie Conrad was over the phone, and her strong personality immediately intimidated me. My lower back was hurting from waiting tables six days a week and Emilie's movement class was recommended to me for relief.

When Emilie invited me to attend her early morning Jungle Gym class, I was thrilled to attend my first class, but I hardly understood a word she said. The vocabulary she used to describe the body was profound and intriguing. Then, when she moved her body to demonstrate nonlinear movement, I was stunned. She reminded me of an octopus. Every bone and muscle in her body was an undulation, like a wave. I'd never seen anything like it before that class. Emilie's philosophy is that human beings come from the ocean and carry the liquid body within. She believes a healthy body isn't primarily a fit or toned body, but one that is permeable and fluid. I was enamored by Emilie's wisdom and dynamic style of teaching. I quickly realized she knew things about the body no one else did. Emilie was a pioneer.

Initially, my body was rigid and uncooperative in her classes. I had to train my brain to think and move differently. In time, everything about the body being liquid made sense and became instinctual and natural to me. The more I participated in her courses and practiced fluid movement, her predictions came true; aches and pains dissipated.

We spent a fair amount of time changing our relationship to gravity, which meant we were upside down often in her Jungle Gym classes. A large net hung from the ceiling like a spider web and students hung upside down from it. Once my body felt the release and stretch of hanging upside down, I knew I was in the right place; every cell in my body responded with euphoria doing asymmetrical movements. I felt a greater sense of wellness after her classes, and in time my entire physique changed shape and form.

Bodyworkers, actors, artists, healers, writers, doctors, nurses, teachers, and dancers were just some of the amazing people who attended her classes. We shared insights, experiences, and inspiration as we moved together. Each participant's contribution to the classes affected me in some way. I felt connected to life and people during and after Emilie's classes. I acquired a profound understanding about the body, and in time realized I was learning from a master. I integrated the new knowledge I gained from Emilie's classes with massage clients and as a result, our sessions were enhanced.

Over the years, I attended several of Emilie's Continuum seminars. They were extremely intense week-long retreats that included three days of integrating sound with breath and movement in silence. I was a fast-moving, determined person, but on those retreats I got very still and quiet. It took a certain amount of self-control for me to be that still but the tranquil environment had a holiness to it that I learned to embrace. The tranquil setting was an invitation for healing to take place.

Emilie used to say, "healing is very mysterious." After I had an emotional breakthrough during one of her retreats her philosophy finally made sense to me. Following several days of moving in that sacred setting, years of dammed emotions released. It came from so deep within, nothing could hold it back. I stood in the shower wailing. I wasn't able to articulate the meaning of the emotional release, but afterwards, I knew it came from an undamaged and wholesome place within me. A place within me that I wanted to know. It was a cathartic cleanse. Afterward I felt vulnerable and fragile, like a newborn baby. It wasn't something we worked towards during the retreats; it was a result of the group energy aligned with breath, sound and movement in a safe environment that allowed the opening to occur. Emilie was a teacher, friend, surrogate mother, healer, mentor, and guru to me. I looked forward to her classes because they challenged me intellectually, physically, and spiritually. Her work was another component that laid the foundation for what was to come in my life.

Since I was a devoted student of Emilie's, I began studying epistemics with her husband at the time, Gary David. Understanding the effects words and meanings have on our emotions was subtle but very powerful. Gary's premise was that as a culture we limit expressing ourselves fully because we over identify our feelings with words. I was intrigued by epistemics because I wanted to garner the discipline to observe my emotions rather than react to them. His non-linear perspective helped me better understand that life is so much more than what we initially see, and that thinking beyond what "is," is imperative for expanding personal awareness. With his guidance I also became intimately familiar with the dynamic role emotions played in my life; in particular the viscous cycle of shame. Studying this new paradigm of thought contributed to my broader sense of self containment and self empowerment. But more than learning another perspective on how to interpret the human condition, what I really appreciated about Gary David was his unapologetic passion for life, and his devotion as a teacher. He was unafraid to express his feelings. In my experience it was an uncommon attribute in a man. I respected his courage and commitment. Gary was a deep thinker, fantastic musician, and a very sincere person who lived from a self actualized place. He became a good friend to both

Michael and me. I treasured our friendship, and I called him more than once for direction at pivotal times in my life. His insights were always a revelation.

I was studying acting when I decided to write a short performance piece about my two sisters called, "Fade to Black." Emilie directed the movement part of the performance and Gary directed the voice over. I performed my movement piece with The Los Angeles Women's Theatre Festival. Thanks to Gary and Emilie, that experience was a personal success, one that empowered my life. Often when I triumphed in some area of my life, it was typical of me to call Gary or Emilie to share the positive news. Like parents, I loved them both.

I was surrounded by brilliant teachers and healers and took comfort in their wisdom and advice. Always a seeker, I was in search of my next spiritual step. Dr. Michael Beckwith, founder of Agape, was just gaining popularity when I discovered his weekly gatherings. Friends raved about his spiritual services. With the Catholic church teachings behind me, I wasn't interested in dogmatic religion anymore, so finding Agape was perfect timing. The first service I attended was riveting. I was surrounded by people living with positive enthusiasm. Exuberance for life permeated the room. There was a palpable sense of joy and passion in the music as well as in almost every person in the service. Hearts were wide open. It was a sharp contrast to the church worship services I had experienced growing up. Agape's focus on meditation, cosmic laws, visioning, and universal principles was another answered prayer.

I also had the opportunity to participate in sweat lodges at The Wright Ranch in Malibu. The ceremonial aspect of the lodges was a deeply rewarding spiritual experience for me. Inside the dark lodge where hot rocks emitted heat, we said prayers and sang songs. The group energy amplified the healing potential in the room and together we purged toxins, lifted our spirits, expanded our awareness, and opened our hearts. I remember coming out of the lodge, lying on the ground, and gazing at all the stars in the sky. Driving home, I felt lighter, as if I was more connected to the universe.

I've always admired people who come into life knowing fully who they are, for me it was never a clear path. Growing up, I felt different from my family, friends, community, and church, and instead of celebrating my originality, I did everything I could to fit into their personal versions of me. As a result, I developed a pattern of looking for love in all the wrong places. It was a pattern that haunted me for many years.

Digging up past traumas wasn't something I anticipated doing when I first moved to California, but once I understood I used food, alcohol, and drugs to forget and avoid. I had to let past events and personal injuries into my conscious awareness, if I truly wanted to heal. Essentially I had to learn to reparent myself.

I was working with a therapist when the reasons for the addictions, depression, and dysfunctional relationships were actualized. In therapy, I came face to face with a tremendous amount of anger about my past. The list of disappointments and betrayals were significant. It was amazing to me how much I buried underneath binging and using drugs, but now that I was sober, there was no place to hide. My desire to heal my life became my priority, so I retreated from my family with a long sabbatical. Relinquishing my relationship with my sisters wasn't easy. I was very close to them and suddenly we lived like strangers. I missed very important events in all of their lives. It wasn't that I didn't love or care about my family; I did. It was more about my quest to be myself and find my voice, no matter what. Differentiating from them was a painful, courageous step, one that I took with a tremendous amount of guilt in the beginning. But a sabbatical was the only course I knew to recover my true self. I was so fortunate to be surrounded by gifted healers, solid friendships, and my incredible husband, Michael, during that time of my life.

Committing to a twelve-step program steered the direction of my life in a positive way. The group consciousness became like family to me, and I was at home in meetings. The steps laid a foundation for personal growth and strengthened my integrity. The support of so many caring people and the mentoring from a sponsor gave me the courage to believe in myself, and in my recovery. AA is one of many bridges I crossed in an effort to redirect my life. I was sober five years when I realized my life was quickly expanding beyond AA principles. Deep into the healing arts, I no longer felt the need to talk about my past. It wasn't like I wanted to erase or deny past events, I just wanted to stop identifying with them. Labeling myself as an alcoholic or addict no longer fit who I had become. I wanted to focus more on where I was going, rather than where I had been. Everything inside me wanted to move forward.

The problem was that I had a lot of fear about leaving the twelve steps. More than once in meetings I heard people say, "Once an alcoholic, always an alcoholic." Every time someone voiced that false premise, I felt defeated and questioned why I felt unique. But the real truth was, at the very core of my being, healing had occurred. The desire or temptation to abuse myself with alcohol or drugs was gone. It was time for me to move forward in my life. With the help of a therapist and Mara Sanders, a wise friend, I summoned the courage to leave the twelve step program but I continued to use many of the tools given to me in those meetings. In particular, the "Serenity Prayer."

"God grant me the courage to accept the things I cannot change, the courage to change the things I can, and the wisdom to know the difference."

This short but insightful prayer is a simplistic but effective tool I use to garner clarity when circumstances in my life feel unmanageable.

The Italian restaurant I worked at was a hot spot for the entertainment business. A lot of famous people came through those doors. Tom Cruise, Daryl Hannah, Michael Penn, Beau Bridges, Sally Fields, Goldie Hawn, Tom Jones, Harvey Korman, Al Pacino, Dustin Hoffmann, Brad Pitt, Denzel Washington, Jackson Browne, Nicole Kidman and many more. Being a Midwestern gal, I was star struck.

The crew of servers were mostly artists and almost all of us were transplants from another state. I gravitated to the gay waiters because they were hysterically funny and original. I spent a lot of time with Chris who was from the East Coast. He was very dramatic, had a great sense of humor and he was a blast to be around. I also became good friends with Jen, an actress with a great personality and a sweet gentle disposition. Her lighthearted nature was uplifting.

In the early days of waiting tables together, it wasn't Michael who interested me as much as his friend and our coworker, Jean Pierre. Jean Pierre was a French photographer, tall, fiery, energetic, and crazy. Naturally, I was intrigued by him and developed a terrible crush. But he was way out of my league for an inexperienced girl from the Midwest. There was no way I could have kept up with that crazy Frenchman's pace. He was older, and he knew exactly what he wanted from women.

With my energy focused on Frenchie, I hardly noticed a sweet Hispanic guy who complimented my blue eyes. Shortly after returning to work from my sister's funeral, Michael very kindly asked me where I had been. His concern sort of shocked me. I wasn't used to compassionate men, and I was surprised he noticed I was gone. I'd worked at the restaurant a very short time before Kim's accident. I'm certain he was the only person who noticed I missed a week of work due to my sister Kim's funeral.

I was terribly nervous around Michael because he was soft spoken. He rarely said anything negative about people and he was comfortable in his own skin. I wasn't comfortable around quiet people, but he grew on me. A good listener with a distinct sensitivity, Michael was solid and strong in ways I hadn't experienced yet in my life. His confidence made him easy to like. In addition his temperament was steady and cool. I was drawn to his tenderness, his compassion and his beautiful brown skin. He had an intensity in his brown eyes, and his hair was long, black and shiny. Often when I looked at him I saw a resemblance of a Native American man. Michael was stunning. Back then he was into lifting weights at Venice Beach, playing sports, reading books, watching films, and studying to be an actor. He was all about living easy on the coast.

I had a strong fear of intimacy and insisted we take our time getting to know one another, and he readily agreed. We eased our way into each others lives. We went on trips, explored in nature, enjoyed long conversations on the beach, and worked together. I knew he could be with almost any woman he chose, but he was with me. Sometimes I felt worthy of his attention and other times I didn't understand what he saw in me. In psychotherapy, I tried to uncover the faulty premises I harbored about my worthiness and my possessive nature.

When we first began dating he lived in a party house with a group of guys in Venice Beach. My friend Chris went to a few of their parties with me. Being sober, Chris and I stood in the corner, smoked cigarettes, and watched everyone get drunk. I had no interest in using alcohol or drugs to fit in with anyone. That destructive phase of my life was over so naturally those parties were short lived for me.

In time, Michael decided our relationship was more important than partying until dawn so he moved out of the party house. In 1991 we escaped the city and rented our first house together in Topanga Canyon.

Our first addition after we moved in together was a puppy. Miles was a rambunctious Dalmatian that brought us pure joy. He strengthened our home life and taught us a few things about ourselves. I was used to having animals around as a kid, but none of them compared to Miles. He was fierce, willful, smart and a great hiking companion. His protective nature insulated me more than once from uncertain people and random rattlesnakes in the canyon where we lived. Much to my surprise, I credit that crazy Dalmatian for teaching me a thing or two about unconditional love.

Michael and I were together five intense, incredible years when he asked me to marry him. Before Michael, I never really considered marriage. I didn't grow up dreaming about finding a husband and getting pregnant. I had other interests. I wanted to explore and see the world. I dreamed of moving to Africa to live like the woman who fostered the lion in the film "Born Free". I enjoyed my freedom and thought having kids and being married would change that. In truth, I also didn't feel I had the temperament to be a good mother. I wasn't born a nurturer. It's a learned behavior I acquired over time, and it wasn't until later in our marriage, after I had a miscarriage, that I felt capable of having a child.

We prepared for the commitment of a lifetime with Camille Maurine and her husband Lorin Roche, meditation teachers. Thanks to them, our wedding was unconventional and unique. We wrote our own vows and planned our wedding with a sweet simplicity. I found my dress in a boutique shop on Montana Avenue in Santa Monica. It was unpretentious and comfortable. Aunt Jo gave me a vintage necklace with matching earrings from her side of the family. The sandals I chose gave me the feeling of going barefoot, which was perfect for our outdoor celebration under the oak trees. I invited Jen, my good friend from the restaurant, and Lynette, a friend from movement class to be in the ceremony. Both were like sisters to me.

It was odd planning one of the main events of my lifetime without my mother or sisters by my side, but I was still trying to make peace with the past. Inviting my family weighed heavily on my mind for some time. In the end, my sister Erin and my Auntie Jo were the only family members present. I invited Emilie Conrad and her teaching partner Susan Harper, as well as Kristy, and Barbara, and other close friends from the Continuum Studio. I cherished those women. In a sweet way, their presence closed the gap of my absent mother and sisters.

It was a very laid-back casual celebration on Summer Solstice in 1995, a beautiful summer day. Michael's family came from Texas as well as a number of friends from the restaurant, and of course our dog Miles. In a circle under the oak trees we gathered to proclaim our love. I remember nearly every detail about that day. It was a glorious beginning to an incredibly powerful relationship. What made me think that marriage and I would not fit?

An Earthquake and A Thief

We were renting a house in Topanga Canyon when the 1994 NorthRidge earthquake struck Los Angeles. At 3:00 a.m., a strong current shook the house and our bed and we woke up, startled. Our dog Miles and every coyote in that canyon howled in the dark black night. It was immediately evident to us that something big had shifted. Fortunately, the house withstood the magnitude of the quake. That left us a bit clueless about the damage done outside of the mountains. Later that morning, when I attempted to drive into Beverly Hills to do a massage at The Peninsula Hotel, large boulders blocked roadways and Pacific Coast Highway was vacant. People stood in lines outside a local grocery store on Sunset Boulevard to try and purchase batteries and water. When I realized Los Angeles was shut down I turned around and headed back home where I immediately began contacting friends to make sure they were safe. We were extremely appreciative our home was intact. Many others weren't as fortunate.

A few weeks after the earthquake, the energy of the city was still fragmented and unsettled. I was on my way to visit a friend after an early morning workout with Emilie Conrad at the Continuum Studio. As I turned onto my friends street, I noticed a man in an alley approaching an elderly woman. Suddenly he pushed the woman down, grabbed her purse, jumped into her car and sped up the alley. I was shocked and furious at his actions. She screamed for help and a neighbor assisted her so I took off behind the stolen car. I followed closely behind the thief and I was tight on his trail. When he noticed he had company, he tried to lose me but I was bold and stayed on him. It was evident he had no plan and no idea where he was going. At one point we pulled up to a stoplight on Ocean Avenue and I rolled down my window and asked two men in a utility truck to help me stop the man in the stolen car. Initially they thought I was nuts, but I quickly explained the situation. Old woman, stolen purse, stolen car ... they got it and joined me in my pursuit.

We drove north on Pacific Coast Highway towards Pacific Palisades, and the driver made a left turn into a subdivision. As it turned out, it was a neighborhood with homes on a cliff overlooking the Pacific Ocean. A few of the homes were in a very precarious state because of the recent earthquake, some were empty and looked ready to tumble off the hillside. The National Guard was there to protect the abandoned houses. It was perfect. I yelled out to the men in uniforms to stop the man in the blue stolen car. The next thing I knew, the National Guard soldiers drew their guns and the two men in the utility truck pulled behind him and blocked his escape route. Police arrived within seconds. The thief came out with his hands in the air. Before I knew it a reporter was on the scene.

Friends thought I was insane to jeopardize my life by following the thief in the stolen car, but I'm assured if they had witnessed an elderly woman being violated they would have responded just the same as me.

A few days later, I received a phone call from the owner of the car. She was thrilled to have her car and purse returned to her. She invited me to dinner with family and friends. It was a delicious dinner and a heartwarming evening at her apartment. Her family rewarded my efforts with a check for $500, which was a complete surprise. Later on, I appeared in court to identify the man.

Running from Fire and Living Coastal

We treasured living in the quiet setting of the Santa Monica Mountains. Shortly after we moved there I found an opportunity to work with horses again. In exchange for taking care of them when the owner traveled out of town, I received a small stipend and I could ride as much as I wished. It was perfect for him and for me.

One warm Indian summer fall afternoon I was riding Sonny, a high-spirited quarter horse, by myself through the canyon. We turned a corner on our way back down the canyon and I smelled fire. Sonny's ears went back and his pace picked up. As soon as we got back to the stables, I unsaddled Sonny, and a smoke-filled sky hovered above us. Red Rock Canyon was on fire.

The canyon was super dry and the fire spread rapidly. It was the first wildfire I'd witnessed and it terrified me. As firemen swarmed the valley, I raced back to our house to get Michael. The smoke grew thick and heavy. In no time at all, the stagnant smoky air smothered each breath we took. Naturally residents were requested to vacate their homes. I called the owner of the horses and told him about the fire and evacuations. He phoned a neighbor and asked him to let the horses out of their corral. He was certain they would take care of themselves and get to safe ground. I was relieved he had a plan. Michael and I gathered a few personal things, our dog Miles, and escaped the threatening fire. We drove to Santa Monica and stayed with our friend Chris from work.

The next three days we watched the Santa Monica Mountains burn from a distance. Several homes were lost in that fire along with thousands of acres. Fortunately, firemen secured the side of the canyon that we lived on. Once again, we escaped danger without physical or financial injuries, but after the earthquake and the fire, I began to understand that the West Coast is an unpredictable place.

Thanks to a coworker at the restaurant, we found a rent-controlled apartment in Santa Monica. The area was gaining popularity and new developments were going up on every corner. And with that, rents were getting steeper. Rent-controlled apartments weren't easy to come by. Even though we knew we would really miss living in Topanga Canyon, we sensed coming down the mountain was right. Our lives were getting very busy and driving back and forth from the canyon wasn't working out for us. Our new apartment was small and funky with neighbors on each side of us. The tight quarters were a trade off because the location was excellent.

We developed a ritual of shopping at the Santa Monica farmers market every Wednesday. We packed our cooler with organic strawberries, spinach, lettuce, avocados, tomatoes, carrots, cabbage, oranges, apples, figs, peaches, apricots, broccoli, radishes. You name it, someone was growing it. Rain or shine, we were there. We loved the interaction with the farmers and the fresh food. The last I heard, at least 10,000 people shop at that Wednesday market. Farmers come from all over Southern California. Chefs often arrive early to get the premier picks of the day. Nestled near the Santa Monica Promenade and the ocean, that farmers market was one of our favorite things about living in the city of Santa Monica.

Life in the city was filled with new routines. Michael walked to work, we rode our bikes on the bike path along the coast from Santa Monica to Marina Del Rey, and we also discovered a few hiking trails nearby in the Santa Monica Mountains. We took Miles hiking on weekends and in between work and classes. Emilie's Continuum studio was becoming more of a second home to me and my new commute was less than ten minutes.

For a short time, I worked at a family-owned Italian restaurant in Malibu. What was great about that job was the small beach town feeling, the famous people who frequented the restaurant, the fantastic menu, and the tips. That Italian restaurant was a quarter of the size of my previous restaurant job and a lot more intense and demanding. I worked lunches, went swimming at Pepperdine University on my break, and then returned for the dinner shift. I was sort of a mad woman, working and moving all the time, but I loved what I was doing.

"Me at Sony Pictures Studios Culver City California." 1999

Rita Hayworth and Acting

After the Italian restaurant in Malibu, I was hired as lead hostess at The Rita Hayworth Dining Room at Sony Pictures Studios in Culver City. I liked the job right from the start. It was a union-paid day position with benefits. I booked lunch reservations for Sony executives; we referred to them as "the suits." Being the captain of the ship, I was the first person everyone spoke to when they entered the dining room. The seating arrangement was very political, certain executives sat only in booths, no tables. I had to be very diligent about the pecking order. Often there was a lot of last-minute juggling. I enjoyed the challenge of keeping everyone happy with their seat and their food.

Over the four years I worked there, a multitude of different actors frequented the studio for lunch, which made a very easy job interesting. It's impossible for me to remember every actor who dined at The Rita Hayworth Dining Room, but I do recall a few—Billy Bob Thornton, Quincy Jones, Catherine Zeta Jones, Antonio Banderas, Tony Danza, Melanie Griffith, Barbara Streisand, Diane Keaton, Sean Connery, Mel Brooks, Ann Bancroft, James Brooks—and so many more.

There was a period of time when Steven Spielberg and Sir Anthony Hopkins ate lunch together. Sir Anthony Hopkins was one of my favorite actors. One afternoon, after I led them to their private booth, I abandoned all self-restraint, I took a deep breath and softly recited to Anthony Hopkins why his flawless performance in the film "Shadowlands" opened my heart. He smiled and thanked me. Then he motioned to Steven Spielberg and said, "What about this guy?"

I said, "Yes, of course, he's amazing too but you have to know, for me, it's you! You're an incredible artist with the ability to transform every character you play. "You're brilliant." Steven Spielberg agreed and Sir Anthony Hopkins stood up and kissed me. I almost fainted! Then, I floated across the dining room back to my position as gatekeeper. I never crossed that professional boundary with any other actor who joined us for lunch at The Rita Hayworth Dining Room. Sir Anthony Hopkins was irresistible.

I was deep into movement classes with Emilie Conrad when she encouraged me to take an acting class. Whether I ever got an acting job out of it or not, she was convinced it would serve my life in a number of different ways. Driving across the country from Ohio to California, I never once dreamt of becoming an actress. Initially I was drawn to the West Coast because of the weather, but the longer I lived in the City of Angels, incredible interesting opportunities continued to come my way.

Michael was already involved in community theatre, and he had an agent and a few commercials under his belt. Once I told him how much I enjoyed the acting classes I discovered, he joined me. We spent the next five years studying "Method Acting" at Paramount Studios in Hollywood with Catlin Adams.

When Catlin was younger, she was an assistant to Lee Strasberg at the Actors Studio in New York City. She was a very passionate, fearless acting teacher. Her classes were rich and personal. She had actors use sense memory as one exercise to get to the heart of characters. It was an exercise where the actor used personal memories to provoke specific emotions for a scene. Sometimes it was a brilliant choice, and other times it was semi-dangerous or inappropriate. Either way, Catlin knew how to get actors to the heart of their characters.

Since I had no formal training before Catlin, it took time to get up to speed with other actors in the class. Some of them were naturals, born to act. The first scene I nailed was from "Bonnie and Clyde." I rehearsed day and night to get to the heart of that character and when I finally did, I understood fully why people became actors. Taking on a character's life, ideas, habits, and emotions was fascinating. You forget about yourself and step into a different reality. It was an exhilarating feeling.

Auditioning for parts was a whole different story for me. That part of the business requires alligator skin. At that time in my life I was trying to change the pattern of appearing tough and invulnerable, so it was a bit of a contradiction for me. I learned, however, to feel less and less self-conscious in Catlin's class, but I never found acting to be easy. It's an art that requires talent, devotion and detailed attention.

Reunited and Transplanting Hope

In 1997, my sister Erin decided to get married. At that point I had been on sabbatical from my family for several years. The last time we were together as a family was our sister Kim's funeral in 1990. Being out of the details of my sisters lives was unsettling, but that was about to change. My family was traveling to the West Coast for Erin's wedding. I was pleased we were reuniting in celebration of something much more positive and I couldn't wait to meet Amy and Blair's daughter, Chelsey. I missed the first five years of Chelsey's life, and I was eager to make up for lost time. Erin's wedding was outside in a beautiful part of the Santa Monica mountains, not far from where Michael and I were married.

Erin continued the pattern of diversity in our family by marrying Javier, from Peru. I appreciate the variety of ethnicities in my family. Amy married Blair, an African American. Kerry married Vaheed from Iran, and of course I'm married to Michael who is Hispanic.

There was a hesitancy in all of us at the ceremony as we slowly warmed up to one another. It was amazing how many years had passed and how everyone of us had changed, yet not changed. I no longer felt like the "baby" of the family, and I was certain healing had take place because my heart was wide open. I was happy to be reunited with my family and I quickly became fond of my new niece. Chelsey was angelic and embodied an exquisite sweetness. There was something in the nature of her spirit I immediately adored. I saw firsthand the bond between Amy and Chelsey. They shared a deep regard for one another, and as mother and daughter, they glowed.

At the same time, after many years of not seeing one another I noticed my sister was pale, thin and had a constant sniffle. Mom said she complained about feeling tired a lot, and she was experiencing nose bleeds at the drop of a hat. I didn't put it all together until a few weeks later when I received a phone call that Amy had been diagnosed with leukemia. I was standing in the kitchen of our apartment when Mom told me the news. My heart sank. I felt instant remorse for missing so many years of her life, but there was no use looking back. Instead, I made a commitment to do anything I could to help save my sisters life. I knew she had many options, and I took it upon myself to show her what some of them were. I knew a lot of healers in California who offered options for dealing with cancer in a more integrated, unconventional fashion and I invited Amy to talk with some of these gifted people. My intention was to encourage her to explore as many options as possible before making any permanent decisions about treatment. I knew she was only familiar with conventional medicine.

The disease came on fast. This was before cancers were so rampant in our society. Statistics were shaky, but people were pulling through the illness. The good news was that our sister Kerry was a perfect match for Amy's bone marrow transplant. Kerry lived with her husband and son in Laguna Niguel, California, and traveled back to Ohio to be Amy's donor. Everyone hoped and prayed for Amy to live.

I went home to Ohio to help guide Amy's treatment choices. It had been a long time since we were friends, and supporting her was my priority. I took her to one of her appointments and when I met her oncologist, I was unimpressed with him. He told Amy having cancer was like being chased by the bogeyman; in order to survive, she had to run for her life. It took everything in me not to stand up and shake him. The last thing a cancer patient needs is a fearful image of their condition. My sister was terribly vulnerable, and his fear-based attitude only made matters worse. Amy deserved better.

I knew I had to find a way to get Amy to consider other treatment options. If I could get her alone then, like the old days, we could have a heart to heart conversation. As a teenager, I had a habit of venturing into her room and confiding my deepest secrets to her. Often those conversations went late into the night. Now in her living room, we talked and giggled like old times. The afternoon was filled with nostalgia. She talked about her daughter Chelsey and how much she loved being a mom. I shared my California lifestyle with her, confided things about my marriage and told her how wonderful life was sober. Every spring when it was warm enough, we skipped school to lay out in the warm sunshine. We lathered ourselves with Johnson baby oil, spread out on foil and baked our bodies until they fried. The sun was a source of nourishment after long cold Ohio winters, and our concern for skin cancer was nonexistent in those days. We laughed about our concert days, when we were enamored with Rick James, Prince, The Time, George Benson, The Gap Band, Luther Vandross, Bob Seger and many other bands.

We reminisced about our trip to Europe when Amy and I had joined the travel abroad group at the small college I attended. It was a short but educational spring break vacation. We visited Paris, Rome, and Pisa with a proficient tour guide and a great group of women. We visited the Louvre, the Eiffel Tower, the Sistine Chapel, The Roman Forum surrounded by ruins, and the Tower of Pisa. Paris was Amy's favorite city. We ate fantastic food and danced our hearts out in nightclubs with friendly Europeans. Our tour bus drove the coastline to Nice where the sea views were enchanting. By the time we got back to Ohio, we were exhausted and worn out, but deeply inspired by our adventure.

We talked for several hours. By the end of our discussion, she agreed to get a second opinion, and the following day I took her to an M.D. who was also an acupuncturist. He was referred to me through a good friend and he was direct with his advice."Have the surgery at The Cleveland Clinic." I was relieved. I knew a team of experts was crucial for my sister's survival.

On my way to the airport in my rental car the song "Amy" by Pure Prairie League played on the radio and my heart skipped a beat. The timing of that song was auspicious. At the airport I called my Aunt Jo in Cleveland. She raved about the Cleveland Clinic and shared success stories of people she knew. When Amy mentioned the Cleveland Clinic to our parents, the thought of her temporarily relocating to Cleveland was too much for them to consider, they thought it was unnecessary and inconvenient for her to travel out of town for surgery. Leaving their comfort zone was never easy for them, but Amy's life was at stake. It was this kind of nonsense that infuriated me about my family and exactly what set me apart from them. Their inability to think beyond conventional advice disappointed me. I was so angry at their lack of support, I wondered if I had made the right decision to be involved with them again. I knew her doctors at Jewish Hospital also had a hand in her decision to stay in Cincinnati for the surgery. It's a strange thing that happens with people when they get sick; suddenly instincts get shut down and the doctors' opinions become the Word of God. Decisions become fear-based. When I got the bad news that Amy decided to stay in Cincinnati for the transplant, I regretted leaving her side too soon.

I wasn't the only one in our family who flirted with an eating disorder. Growing up, Amy exercised a lot and got very rigid about what she could and could not eat. That pattern was still active in her as a mother, and before she entered the hospital for the transplant she was very thin, too thin. She was also extremely stressed out. Her husband, Blair was traveling a lot, which was hard on their marriage. She discovered he had affairs on the road and the news if his betrayals broke her heart. No matter how much we encouraged her to take the focus off of Blair so that she could reclaim her health, she couldn't. He was the love of her life before her daughter Chelsey was born. Cancer or no cancer, she was obsessed with saving their marriage.

I slept at the hospital with Amy after her surgery. Although unconscious, I sensed she knew I was in that room. Her heart rate accelerated whenever I spoke to her. I massaged her, caressing her war-torn arms, bruised from all the needle poking. I reaffirmed over and over to her that she wasn't alone. I could tell she knew someone who loved her was within reach because of her subtle responses. With no extra reserves in her body to withstand such an invasive surgery, her recovery was bleak. At first her bone marrow transplant appeared to be a success, but in time her recovery was not what we had hoped, and because it was a teaching hospital, I felt Amy was treated more like an experiment than a person whose fate was on the line. With the exception of a few concerned nurses who cared for her, that hospital was cold, uninviting, and lifeless. The gap between practicing medicine and compassionate consideration for a patient's survival was palpable. I would have given anything to take her home.

It would be impossible for me to count all the times Amy came to my rescue when I was a child. She covered for me at home when I skipped school or stayed out all night with friends. She took me to the food doctor in an effort to stop my binging, she let me borrow money when I was broke, then gave me a job at the comedy club she owned. When I was four years old she beat up our neighbor for breaking my arm by running over it with his bike. She drove me to OA meetings, listened to my problems and offered solutions. She intervened in my life when I was lost and confused. She was a great friend and sister.

I was working at The Rita Hayworth Dining Room when I got the call about Amy's decline. I scheduled a flight to Ohio the following day. On the airplane, I focused hard on seeing my sister alive one final time. But the closer we got to the Midwest, the more I knew I was too late. On the airplane I felt something flutter in my body: a light lift, and then a subtle release. I sensed Amy died while the airplane I was on was in the air. At the airport, my older sisters Erin and Pam waited for me at the gate. I knew immediately Amy was dead by the look on their faces.

Burying Amy was harder than burying my sister Kim because of Chelsey, her daughter. Chelsey was only six years old when her mom died. No matter how many adults encouraged Chelsey to see her mom laid out inside the church, she refused. It was a wise choice for such a young child. I applauded her instincts and intuition. Her mom was barely recognizable, the cancer treatments made her look old, grey, and worn out. She was blown up like a stuffed doll. Her face was covered with cheap makeup, a ritual I find appalling. I intended to support and encourage Chelsey through her life now that her mother was gone. After everything Amy did for me, it was the least I could do for her.

I returned to California devastated. The grief I felt was insurmountable. My second sister was gone, and part of me with her. I took a few days off work and confined myself to our apartment, where I reviewed childhood photos and old letters. Emilie Conrad, my friend and mentor then, called to check on me. When I explained I could hardly function outside of the apartment, she informed me I was sitting Shiva. It was the first time I'd heard that term. In the Jewish tradition, those grieving don't leave home for a week. It's a sensitive and sacred time for the family members of the deceased. Visitors are welcomed, but conversation is kept to a minimum. Emilie was right. I was sitting Shiva for Amy. When friends stopped over, I appreciated their kind words but I had nothing to give. I secluded myself until I felt capable of returning to my every day life.

A Culprit and A Quest

When I was in high school, I was diagnosed with mononucleosis. Our family doctor ordered me to stay in bed and rest, but missing a good party back then didn't sit well with me. I paid little attention to the diagnosis and dismissed the advice of the doctor. After saying goodnight to my parents, I put on a dress, threw my shoes out the window, climbed down our chimney, and made a beeline for friends' parties. Nothing came in between me and a good time.

In California, I was worried mono had come back to haunt me. I was having symptoms of chronic fatigue and for the first time in my life I was unable to sleep soundly. Insomnia made everything feel daunting, including driving in traffic in Los Angeles.

A few people thought I was burning the candle at both ends. Maybe they were right. I kept a tight, busy schedule, with very little down time. I worked out before my daytime job at The Rita Hayworth Dining Room, and sometimes after work, too. Evenings were spent taking acting class or massaging clients. Weekends I hiked, socialized and scheduled more massages. I pushed myself to keep going because I couldn't sit for long periods without feeling life was passing me by. I was slightly manic, with Type-A tendencies. The truth was I felt most alive when I was achieving or working toward a goal, but my obsessive-compulsive behavior was exhausting my body.

I could no longer walk our dog Miles around the block because I felt weaker every day. It seemed like my entire being was repulsed by city life. My body started to react to everything—perfume, cologne, cigarettes, paint, detergents, bleach, gas—anything synthetic with a chemical base. If I was exposed to strong scents, like exhaust fumes, a migraine would surface immediately, and I'd be afflicted with brain fog and dizziness. My immune system was totally overwhelmed. Eventually I would learn that this condition is called Multiple Chemical Sensitivities or MCS.

My logical mind wanted answers. I wondered if doing massage was the culprit. I really enjoyed working with clients but often I felt drained after appointments. I thought maybe I needed to protect myself with clearer boundaries, and be more conscious of not taking clients' unresolved issues on. Then I thought I just needed to rest so I tried living with Buddhists at a retreat center in the mountains for a month. I left early when heart palpitations were so severe I thought I might have a heart attack during during one of the meditations. When I returned home the heart palpitations continued. One evening they were so severe Michael took me to the emergency room. The emergency staff treated me like I was on amphetamines and sent me home without answers. Their lack of compassion disgusted me. After that I insisted I was finished with Allopathic medicine.

I was relieved when a friend recommended a nutritionist in Seattle. Following a lengthy phone conversation with her I felt she understood my health challenges. She was compassionate and committed to finding answers, so I flew to Seattle for an appointment with her. A diet of high fats, protein, and no wheat or gluten was recommended by her as well as additional testing with other alternative practitioners. The naturopath and chiropractor she worked with diagnosed me with "possible" mercury poisoning and Lyme's Disease. Tests also indicated my adrenal glands were exhausted. Too weak to work, I returned to Los Angeles, quit my job, and put all my energy into my health crisis.

I convinced myself the next step was to remove my eight amalgam fillings because they had mercury. An affordable biological dentist in Tijuana came highly recommended to me, so Michael and I traveled to Mexico to meet him. We learned people traveled from all over the U.S. to have specific dental procedures performed only by Dr. Villafaña, and we quickly understand why. He was so much more than a dentist. He had the hands and the heart of a healer. He was calm, present, and extremely informed. We were confident Dr. Villafaña was the right dentist for the invasive oral procedure.

The trips to Tijuana were exhausting for me, but I was intent on removing the mercury and restoring my health as quickly as possible. I took the train to San Diego, then I took the trolley to the border, I walked across the border, then took a cab to his office. On those long trips down south, Michael had to work, so I traveled alone. Some days I was super weak and could hardly walk from the parking lot to the train depot. A few times I nearly fainted in line waiting at the border to get back across to San Diego.

It took several months to remove the amalgam fillings. Shortly afterwards someone suggested my health issues were identical to a person exposed to mold. It wasn't the first time I'd heard about people suffering from sick building syndrome or mold toxicity in Santa Monica. Our apartment complex was close enough to the beach to give mold the right environment to grow. We lived in our rent-controlled apartment because it was inexpensive, and it was in a great location. The modest rent gave us the financial freedom to travel, take classes, save money, and pursue other interests. The downside to our apartment though was that it was an old neglected building. Being a rent controlled property the landlord couldn't raise rents, so she avoided doing any kind of renovations. Hardwood floors needed refurbishing and doors, windows and appliances needed upgrading. In truth, the whole building needed a cleanse. Nonetheless, we painted it, replaced the kitchen and bathroom floors, and made it comfortable.

I continued to research mold toxicity and once I knew what it looked like, I found it growing in our apartment. Michael and I were unsuccessful removing it, so we informed the landlord of the mold. She thought we were exaggerating the problem and had no intentions of rectifying it. Around that time a lot of tenants were suing landlords for toxic mold exposures, but I had no desire to go down that path. I just wanted to feel better.

We quickly learned treating mold toxicity in people was challenging. There's no magic pill to eradicate symptoms and although it was evident to us that we needed to move, we couldn't see where to yet. I was spending a lot of money on alternative solutions and doctors, and if we moved; we faced steep rents. We didn't see how we could pay more in rent and continue to seek alternative medical advice and treatment. Plus, the exposure had already occurred. We didn't want to think it was too late, but the damage to my health was already done. We were left between a rock and a hard place.

By this time I had been on a healing path for awhile and I was aware enough to know that body, mind, and spirit are all connected. It occurred to me more than once that what was going on inside my heart and mind was clearly manifesting physically. I was doing the best I could navigating my way through daily life, but I still struggled with trusting my instincts. I took the advice of my mentors before my own innate guidance, always reaching outside of myself for answers or approval. I also lived with an active inner critic and as a result; I was very hard on myself and others. I was a people pleaser and an approval seeker. Those patterns were ingrained since childhood and at times felt impossible for me to eradicate. It's likely the combination of living in the mold along with the inner restlessness within were the perfect combination for failed health. Michael's constitution was much stronger than mine. He became somewhat sensitive after the exposure. Fortunately he escaped the more severe ramifications.

Often when things get uncomfortable in our lives, Michael comes up with a great idea. It's one of the many things I adore and admire about him. He has a way of seeing right through problems to solutions. Since it was almost impossible for me to walk around the block, he thought I might feel better if I got out of the city and out of our apartment. I looked into going on retreat at The Esalen Institute in Big Sur, California, but it was out of our price range. Lo and behold, their neighbor wasn't.

The Growing Edge was an incredible retreat house at the edge of the sea, a small piece of refuge in a larger paradise. There was one room left to rent for winter when we contacted the owners, so Michael and I immediately drove up to check it out. When we arrived, we had a meeting with Kaye, the founder, and her partner David. I felt at home with them immediately. The room available to rent was a six month commitment, a lengthy amount of time for me to consider, but I was super weak and had no idea how long it would take for my health to improve. Retreating to the

Growing Edge seemed like the best prescription for rejuvenation. I left Michael and our dog Miles in Santa Monica and headed north to reclaim my health.

I was on my own for the first time in my life, and I embraced the solitude. Instead of checking into a hospital, I checked into nature and I had a front row seat to her incredible display. My tiny room overlooked the ocean where I watched a bevy of dolphins, countless grey whales, sea otters, and red-tailed hawks day after day. Throughout the day, the sun illuminated the sea in fantastic nuances. I took those subtle light variations as signs of something greater, summoning me to reach for the pervasive light. At dusk, when the new moon emerged, her delicate appearance resembled a slight sliver, like a golden banana hanging gently from the sky. It was glorious to be wrapped around nature's gifts on every side. Often I would spend all day with my belly against Mother Earth. I felt like a child resting in the womb. The incredible songs of birds filled my heart. I fell in love with the sweet sea otters flopping around in the Pacific below and the soft ocean breeze that drifted through my tiny bedroom window. Sometimes it seemed like I was on a ship out at sea, waiting for my next destination.

In time, I started to hear and feel the rhythm of my heart beat normal again. I wanted to know what was playing out in my body and spirit. Once again, I knew it wasn't a separate dance. I thought if I could get to a quiet place with fewer distractions, I would be with myself and better understand the bigger picture. I knew it wasn't another teacher, another class or another doctor's prescription that would cure me. I knew the answer was within. Something inside was waiting for my undivided attention.

It took courage to be on my own in a very uncertain time. It was November 2001. A lot was changing in the world, and fear dominated the collective unconscious. I made a commitment to have no connection to the outside world those six months. I didn't have a computer, a T.V. or even a radio. I wrote letters to friends and family, kept a journal, and read book after book on healing. I slept, dreamt, and reflected. I stepped out of life to step in. I wanted to find my voice, not the voice of anyone elses. My voice.

It was the first time I retreated from other people's advice and opinions with confidence. At The Growing Edge, I had no one to please but myself.

The house was rented to interesting people, mostly students at Esalen. Each one of us was trying to reconcile our paths in life. We shared a communal kitchen and great conversations. David and Kaye took their time preparing delicious dinners for themselves almost every evening. It was good for me to witness. Back in Santa Monica, I ate good food prepared mostly by Michael, primarily for fuel. My busy schedule came before everything, including learning to nurture myself by cooking for myself. There really wasn't any reason I couldn't do the same as Kaye and David. I saw firsthand how fresh and nourishing food is a powerful source of medicine.

Kaye and David had dynamic friends who visited. One friend was an astrologer who read charts from an Eastern perspective. My sister Erin studied astrology and had worked on mine and Michael's astrological charts when we were newly married. As it turns out both Michael and I were born on full moons! I found that information helpful because often I have a tremendous amount of energy every month during the cycle of the full moon.

During the reading at Big Sur, the astrologer pointed out how important it is for me to live in close proximity to mountains. There is something about mountains that restores my spirit. It's no wonder I felt at home in Big Sur. I'm certain that was also part of the pull for me to move out West from Ohio. After many years of living around mountains in Santa Monica, I was accustomed to being around them and much more at peace living in their shadows. To this day, I feel uneasy in flat states where I am able to see horizons.

Every now and again I would endure periods when I really missed Michael, my friends, work, Miles our dog, and our social world. It was a vulnerable feeling that challenged my commitment to stay. Other times I thought maybe I was wasting my time because my health wasn't improving at the rate I expected. But then I would remember healing is very mysterious so putting a timeline on my recovery was useless. What got me through my commitment was Julia Butterfly Hill. Around the same time, she sat in an old redwood tree for two years in an effort to stop the logging of the ancient redwoods. I thought of her many times and decided, if Julia could sit for two years, I could sit for six months.

Kaye was the perfect woman to manage the retreat house. Her compassion and integrity went hand in hand. Her closest friend Jackie escaped frigid Canadian winters and stayed in a room at The Growing Edge. As it turned out, Jackie and I discovered we had friends in common in Santa Monica. I had many long conversations with Jackie, and I was impressed when I learned she lived on a 350-acre farm off the grid in Canada. Life on the farm for her was creative, interesting, challenging and peaceful. Jackie's life made impressions on me.

My parents visited once, which really surprised me. They took me out to dinner and drove me to the grocery store in Monterey. It was my first and only trip out of Big Sur the entire six months I lived there. Their visit became another integral part of my healing. We had a heart to heart conversation, and for the first time in my adult life I felt a deep connection to both of them.

David, Growing Edge founder, was a fantastic gardener, and as spring got closer it became a ritual of mine to watch his garden bloom. Spinach, leeks, lettuces, kale, onions, potatoes; healthy gorgeous plants produced fresh food for his evening meals with Kaye. I reveled in his food court on my way out for short walks.

Being a Big Sur resident, I also shared the privilege of soaking in Esalen's hot springs. It took several months before I had the stamina to walk over and use them, but once I did, I made it a point to get in that water as much as possible. The baths relieved my body of stress and filled my mind with hope for health. On my way over, I'd rest at Esalen's exquisite vegetable gardens; that part of the land radiated with life. Watching a crew of apprentices nurture that magnificent creation was inspiring. In Santa Monica, our Wednesday ritual was shopping at the farmers market, but seeing where food originated sparked my desire to cultivate a garden of our own.

The longer I lived in those mountains an environment outside of the city was becoming more and more appealing to me. When Michael visited, fresh air and quiet starry nights caught his attention, too. Together we wondered where and how we might find a similar setting to reside in.

Going away to reclaim my health was a step in the most promising direction. Extreme, but a beginning. My health concerns weren't entirely answered, but I faced a few demons and put out a few fires within. I was taking long walks again, and internally I felt stronger. At the end of six months, I felt certain it was time to take on life again. I was ready to come down from the mountain from my vision quest. So I did.

Returning to the Lights

It was great to be home with Michael and Miles but after six months of living in a peaceful setting, city life no longer appealed to me. With new developments occurring on every corner, Santa Monica was growing louder everyday. In addition, a few new people moved into our apartment building while I was out of town, and they were obnoxious and loud. After living at The Growing Edge surrounded by conscientious roommates, it was hard to tolerate people partying until dawn.

The late-night interruptions continued despite my requests for them to quiet down, so I called the landlord and asked her to address the problem. Her advice was for me to call the police. I thought it was a poor decision on her behalf. The police considered calls of that nature insignificant and sometimes they didn't show up. There were a lot of other, more serious issues that needed their attention, so I took it upon myself to have quiet restored to our building. I went directly to the person who was having the parties and kindly asked her to be more considerate of her neighbors and quiet down. I had no idea that simple request would come back to haunt me.

A few days later I was planting flowers in our garden bed when she confronted me. She was furious with my plea for peace and quiet. It was 2:00 p.m. on a Sunday afternoon, and she was drunk. She got in my face, said some crude vulgar things and went off on a rampage. Before I knew it, she slapped me in the back of the head. It happened so quickly I thought she hit me with a large rock or a brick. I got dizzy and lightheaded. I quickly steadied myself. Her reckless behavior repulsed me but I didn't fight back.

I looked her in the eyes and said, "You just really screwed up." Then I went inside and called the police. Her behavior shocked and alarmed her friends, who were also tenants; they scattered. She stumbled behind after them. The police took a full report and put a detective on the case. Soon enough, we discovered her visa had expired so she was in the country illegally, and she was wanted for a hit and run. Her police record made the landlord nervous because she was considered a liability. Within a week she was evicted. Finding the stamina to deal with petty things like drunk neighbors was not how I wanted to spend my energy. After that incident my desire to live in a different environment grew stronger and stronger every day.

Not long after I put that fire out, I was in a car accident. The worst part about it, I was at fault. I failed to see a fast moving motorcyclist when I pulled out of a parking lot on Ocean Avenue. I was traumatized by the impact of our collision, but it was nothing compared to the motorcyclist's injuries. He was in bad shape. Before I knew it, paramedics, and police were on the scene, and he was taken away in an ambulance. I was advised to go to the hospital but that was the last place I wanted to be, so I declined. I was terribly concerned about the guy I hit, so after the police report was filed, I went home and tried to relax, but it was hard to shake off the incident.

Before the collision I wasn't getting any answers about my health from Western medical doctors so I swore off Allopathic medicine. But that decision was about to change. My left leg had a growth of fatty tissue and although I assumed it was nothing to be alarmed about, after the accident it became problematic because the impact of the collision made it ache. Michael insisted I see a doctor and have it checked out. As much as I didn't want to deal with conventional doctors, I knew Michael was right, so I scheduled an appointment. The following week a young surgeon ran some tests and results indicated first stages of a rare sarcoma cancer. I was totally caught off guard by the diagnosis. I was almost certain he had the wrong person. Then I thought about my two dead sisters. Amy was thirty-seven years old when she died from leukemia, and Kim was thirty-five when she died in a car accident. At the time of the diagnosis, I was thirty-six. Was I next? Suddenly I felt an impending urge to abandon everything and run for my life. But where to? The bad news was amplified when the surgeon said the tumor was in a delicate place; sciatica nerves could get severed and paralysis might result. Basically he couldn't guarantee I'd walk again. Tumor or no tumor, the young surgeon wasn't touching me. I watched my sister Amy die in the hospital, and I wasn't going down the same road.

It took a tremendous amount of energy but the warrior within me came alive. I was concerned for my life and suddenly I felt on fire to hold onto it. It took a great deal of insistence with our insurance company to get a second opinion, but finally with the help of an incredible saintly woman from the insurance agency, I got an appointment with one of the best surgeons at UCLA. It was a miracle.

Dr. Eilber, a UCLA surgeon was a master in his field. I took the x-rays and test results to him for a second opinion, and he didn't even blink after looking at them. His attitude was carefree, easy going and confident. "You gotta get that out," was his response. "I can do it, don't worry about not walking again, it's not an issue, never should have been. The muscle will grow back, you'll be fine." I was aghast at his confidence and thrilled for the reassurance that paralysis wasn't an issue. Standing in his waiting room, I couldn't hold back the tears. For the first time since the diagnosis, my entire body loosened and once again I could breathe deeply. The good news was a huge relief. I was in good hands with the elder surgeon, and my mind and body knew it.

My appreciation for the woman who assisted me with the health insurance details overflowed. I sent her flowers and gift certificates for her committed efforts. She opened a door for me that changed the direction of my recovery and ultimately my life.

What It Was Like

It's 5:00 a.m. We are driving to the hospital. Darkness surrounds us. Most of L.A. sleeps soundly. I am nervous. We arrive at the hospital and wait for admissions to open. The woman next to me in the waiting room talks on a cell phone about her dying mother. I am irritated. It's too damn early to be hearing about death. I imagine running from this place, this surgery, my failing body. Perhaps finding a cure on a faraway island. But I know it's too late to run; the tumor on my leg is too big to just disappear.

Finally, we get through the paperwork with admissions. I undress and they take us downstairs where we wait with about fifteen other patients, each of us in our own bed. Most are watching T.V. I am annoyed: how can they watch T.V. at a time like this? Anything not to be present.

The nurse male starts my preparation. Michael holds my hand. I sign papers admitting we will not sue if I don't wake up from the operation. I am tense. The elder surgeon dances his way over to me. He is wide awake and very happy. I giggle. He tells me I have nothing to worry about. Not one thing. Everything will be perfect. I like his confidence. My nerves settle down. The anesthesiologist starts drilling me about my health. I hesitate to answer. I'm afraid they won't do the surgery if they know how sick I have been, but I want this tumor out of my body today. I answer anyway. Surprisingly, he says I'm healthy compared to most. I can only imagine. They are ready to put me under. I say goodbye to Michael. Our eyes meet. I stroke his face. He kisses me. We push our tears down. Too many people surround us. He squeezes my hand. "I love you," he whispers. I smile. An IV is inserted. A cold rush oozes through my veins. I feel good all over.

I gaze at male nurses beside my bed. They have broad shoulders and confident manners. I love them. They will protect me. Michael's face fades. It is black all around me.

I hear something. There is a person in my face. I don't recognize him. He shouts, "It looks benign." I push my eyes open. He smiles. Oh yes, it's the elder surgeon. "Good news," he says again, "it looks benign." I can't move. Pain creeps up and down my leg. It bangs like a broken door struggling to hang on its hinge in a storm. I try to speak but nothing comes out. My raw throat aches. Who are these strangers next to me covered in white sheets? I see a man wheeling around another body. This place looks like a morgue. I try to awaken. I can't get any words out. Have I lost my voice? I let go and fall back asleep. I wake up in a confused daze. Light surrounds me. There is a glare coming through the dark green window. I can almost see blue skies. Michael is next to me. He holds my hand. I try to stay awake. The pain demands my attention. A nurse comes in. "Push the tiny black button on your chest if you have pain," she shouts. I push it over and over and over until I feel nothing. Michael tells me the good news about the removed tumor. I feel secure again when I hear those words.

I meet my roommate. She is twenty years old and the cancer in her leg came back after being free of it for one year. She cries day and night. Her leg is enormous. They say it is inflamed because the cancer is stopping her blood flow and circulation. When she tells me her name is Amy, I get queasy. Tears roll down my face. Amy was my sister's name. She can't see me, so I continue to cry silently. I can't tell her I had a beautiful sister named Amy who died from cancer. I take a deep breath and listen to her story.

She has a daughter and lives in Bakersfield. Her wedding is scheduled for the spring. She doesn't understand how the cancer came back. She is scared for her life. The pain debilitates her. Her family calls on the phone and she cries to them except when she talks to her daughter, her voice changes. She tries to find strength beneath the relentless fear to comfort her daughter. The nurses are cruel to her. They don't want to be worn thin by her needs. I loathe their attitudes and lack of compassion. Her doctors prescribe antidepressants to calm her fears of death. I wish they would just sit down and listen to her. I want to tell them she is a person, not an experiment. I cry with her when she is not looking.

Friends and family stop by with words of hope and exquisite flowers. I am comforted by their visits. When the physical therapist arrives to assist me in a stroll down the hall, I realize this is the cancer ward. I get angry. I do not belong on this floor. I do not have cancer. How dare they put me with all these sick people? My tumor is benign, dammit. The thoughts continue until I am exhausted. The next morning I awake. The hospital feels like a prison. I have to get out of here. I start to feel crazy. I am not sleeping at night because the nurses poke Amy every two hours and she cries for more painkillers. I demand to go home. The elder surgeon finally permits my release. "I will have the lab results in a week," he says as I am leaving.

One week later, but no answer. He says the results have been delayed due to the Thanksgiving holiday. The nightmares begin. I am running from fire. Everywhere I am haunted by dark creatures and scary images. Bears attack me. Little tiny ferrets bite my face and my body. I begin to feel suspicious. The test results are taking too long. I can't breathe deeply. My instincts tell me I'm in trouble.

Friday finally arrives, and I make the dreaded phone call. I detect hesitancy as soon as I hear the older surgeon's voice. My stomach flips. A deep rush of heat surges throughout my body.

"There's a little," he softly whispers. What does this mean, I ask? "Treatment. We have to put the fire out," he says.

I'm home alone. I start to cry. The walls in our apartment get very narrow, as if they are closing in on me. I sink back into the couch like a wet pillow and disappear inside. I can't feel anything. I look out the window at the birds perched at our bird feeder. I watch them feed a newborn with tenderness as I hang up the phone.

Alternative Medicine and a Train Wreck

Although I sustained several injuries with broken bones and minor accidents as a child, nothing compared to the pain I felt in my leg after the tumor was removed. The first few days at home after the surgery were brutal. Michael took care of everything from working, cooking, walking Miles, running errands to bathing me. In order for me to take a shower, we wrapped my leg in Saran Wrap, then he held me up while I washed. The warm water soothed my entire aching body. It was taxing for me to be so dependent on Michael, but I didn't have a choice. He was incredibly tender and supportive throughout the entire process. I didn't take his strength and devotion for granted. I couldn't wait to get better and live a normal life again.

Since my immune system was weak, I started to have some issues with my teeth. One tooth in particular fell right out of my mouth so I returned to Dr. Villafaña, our dentist in Tijuana for an appointment. When I told him the news about cancer and treatment, he recommended a homeopathic doctor not far from his office. I was very uncertain about doing radiation and thought a second opinion from a non-Western doctor would be helpful.

The homeopathic doctor explained another side of cancer: the political side. In his view, cancer is a business. He said doctors prescribe radiation and chemotherapy even when it wasn't always necessary. Radiation equipment is expensive, and doctors needed patients to help pay for them. It was hard to hear, but I knew where he was coming from. I witnessed my sister Amy's disastrous decline from cancer treatments, some of which seemed totally unnecessary. I felt there was some truth to his convictions. Before I left, he made a very specific homeopathic remedy for my immune system. I started taking it immediately. On the drive back to Los Angeles, I knew the next step wasn't going to be an easy decision for me.

About a week later I discovered a Chinese acupuncturist in Santa Monica who specialized in treating patients with cancer. Dr. Ha and his wife, Ping Ha were the only two people in the alternative medicine world who specifically understood and treated sarcomas. I met with both of them to discuss my treatment options and I was surprised at their advice.

Dr. Ha confessed he couldn't take me on as his patient unless I did both Eastern and Western medicine together. In his opinion the combination of both modalities had more of a chance eliminating cancer cells than one alone. Without doing both, he felt certain the disease would return and it could easily spread to my lungs. Sarcoma's could be relentless. His premise was to catch it in the early stages while we had a window of time. I listened carefully, and thought long and hard about his opinion. His convictions were strong. The thought of the disease spreading or returning was unacceptable to me. I knew people who went back and forth chasing cancer in their bodies, and that wasn't the future I imagined for myself. But after the surgery, I felt even more like a puritan. I didn't want harsh invasive procedures touching my body, my skin, my cells or muscles. I was still weak and wasn't sure I could handle radiation. At the same time, I didn't want to go through another surgery. I was terrified of dying from cancer like my sister Amy and I couldn't believe I was being faced with my mortality at such a young age. I wanted to make the best of whatever decision I made and then get on with living.

After many days of contemplation, I decided to go with Dr. Ha's advice. Dr. Ha and his wife, Ping Ha, became my allies. I integrated acupuncture treatments with radiation sessions four times a week. We spent thousands of dollars on acupuncture treatments. Often I would go right from radiation to their office. Radiation treatments scorched my leg and made me weak and tired, but going straight to his office for a session lifted my spirits and increased my confidence in my recovery. It took time, but I got stronger. The acupuncture increased the blood flow and circulation to my leg, and strengthened my immunity. The Ha's recommended no sugar in my diet and bone broths to strengthen my immune system. I hardly had any appetite and I was super thin. I ate soothing foods, easy to digest, like baby foods. As soon as my gut would allow it, I took Chinese herbs to strengthen my stomach and immune system.

During the six weeks of treatment, I created a "dream wall" in our bedroom. Every time I had a powerful dream, I made a collage to represent what the dream indicated to me. I expected to be informed by my dreams; in fact, like other cultures I relied on them for additional guidance or awareness. I had many dreams about fire. Often I would be running across canyons away from flames. I knew that meant the radiation was squelching cancer's fire. I grew fascinated by my body's ability to repair itself. In time my left leg, although it was never the same, did restore itself. It was about a year before I was able to walk normally again. From the time I initially started feeling sick to the end of radiation, three years had passed and I was in bed that entire time.

The time had come for us to move out of our rent controlled apartment. After searching several months for a place to live we finally found a remodeled bungalow in Venice, California that suited us. It provided us with a little more privacy and no more "shared walls." The rent was more than double what we paid for our rent controlled apartment in Santa Monica, but we decided to commit for a year and then reevaluate things. We moved out of our moldy apartment and never looked back.

A few months after we moved into our new bungalow we received an alarming phone call from Michael's family in Texas early one Sunday morning. Michael was walking our dog, Miles, around the block when I received the call. I sensed immediately something tragic happened because Michael's aunt was crying. It was hard for me to understand exactly what she was saying, but after a few minutes of probing her, I finally got her message. Michael and Miles were making their way up the driveway to our bungalow, their sweet faces after a brisk walk was the last thing I saw as the bad news echoed over the telephone; Frank, Michael's father was dead. Unwanted news about death is like a curse that creeps over you and sucks the life force right out of your body.

The bad news hit us like a train wreck. It seemed like we were just coming up for air from the trauma around the cancer diagnosis and now Michael's father was gone.

Frank was the kind of man who would do anything for his family and friends. He had a gentle spirit and an eagerness to lend a helping hand to almost everyone. Growing up in a poor cotton-picking family, he was one of nine children. He worked hard to put his two sons through college and was proud he created a life outside of poverty for his family. What made Frank's death even harder to swallow was that he took his own life. We wondered long and hard how we didn't see it coming. We felt remorse for being too wrapped up in our lives to be there for Frank.

Michael was totally despondent. I held him in my arms as he grieved. We flew to Dallas from LA for the funeral and he shed tears the entire flight home. I sat close to him and gave him full permission to express himself. A few people sitting near us on the airplane looked concerned about Michael, but their discomfort was the last thing on my mind. Allowing Michael weep for his father was not only right, but also healthy. He loved his father. His heart was broken.

Michael's brother, Jim, was just a few years younger than him. They took different paths in their lives but were still good friends. Not long after Frank's suicide, Jim got mixed up with drugs and was sentenced to eight years in prison. Jim and Frank were two men very dear to Michael, and he lost both of them at the same time. Normally a very stable, grounded man, these two experiences afflicted my sweet husband to the very core. It was the second time in our marriage he was thrown off center. Between my cancer diagnosis, Jim's prison sentencing and Frank's suicide, I was concerned about the state of Michael's mind. I knew he was fragile and on the verge of depression.

We took score of where our lives were and decided it was time for us to do something different. Health or no health, I was alive. If we could do anything at all in our lives, what would it be? The summer before the cancer diagnosis, we visited our friend Jackie from The Growing Edge on her 350-acre farm in Canada. We worked in the garden, ate delicious grass-fed meat, strolled through the countryside and swam in her spring-fed pond.

On that land we felt the pull of Mother Nature: "Come this way." I was certain that kind of lifestyle was summoning us. It was time to make a bold move, time to take a risk. In March 2004 we sold almost everything we owned, loaded our dog Miles into our SUV and we left the City of Angels.

Part Three

King Hill Farm, Maine 2004

We had heard more than once that Maine is a beautiful state. It had been on our radar as a place to explore for a long time. Since we wanted to do something entirely new and different, we looked into an organization called MOFGA (Maine Organic Farmers and Gardeners Association) and we found a farm that appealed to us. In our early thirties we became farm apprentices!

Our commitment to work at King Hill Farm was for ten months. Starting in March and ending in November. I had no idea how I would physically do it, but I knew it was our next step. We arrived in March, the beginning of lambing season. Nurturing precious newborns softened our hearts and restored our spirits. I jumped right in and became the midwife to the sheep.

I spent a few summers working as a camp counselor in college and the housing for counselors was immaculate compared to the apprentice cabin we moved into on King Hill Farm. When we arrived it hadn't been cleaned in almost ten years. We were amazed previous farmhands could live in a place so filthy but soon enough we would learn why. Cobwebs, clutter, dirty stove, tarnished dishpans, soiled oven, old moldy food, and mice, lots of them. Initially our schedule was too demanding to find time to clean, but we were determined to live in a comfortable place. Eventually we painted it and did everything we could to make it feel like home. On Sunday, our day off, we took load after load of junk to the dump.

Instead of a bathroom we had a separate room in the back of the cabin. It was a small space comprised of rocks that made up a shower. Stepping into that small nook to shower was like walking into a cave, and in cold weather it was shocking. The hot water heater was a small tank and worked for less than five minutes. Living without a bathtub was trying for me.

In addition, we shared an outhouse and our small kitchen with Laura, another apprentice who lived in an even smaller cabin, "the love shack," across from us. Like a lot of women who farm, Laura was incredible. She knew how to do just about everything on that farm and she treated it like it was her own. We learned a lot from her. I admired her expertise and fearless attitude.

The farm was spread out over 160 acres and surrounded by water, trees, abundant wildlife and a spring-fed pond that we frequented during growing season. Our commute to the farmhouse and the garden was about seventy five yards, no traffic and very few distractions. Our only phone and computer service was at the main farmhouse. We got dial-up about once a week.

We tended to sheep, lambs, cows, pigs, turkeys, chickens, ducks, rabbits, and a few acres in vegetables. All the animals were on a pasture rotation schedule. During the high season, we also had a booth at The Blue Hill Farmers Market and a CSA (community-supported agriculture) for senior citizens. Our exit out of the city to work that land was the perfect medicine for our troubled hearts.

We weren't accustomed to the long days, working in every climate, and the physical stamina it took to farm, but after a couple of months and a few not-too-serious injuries, our bodies adjusted. In summer, we acclimated to black fly season, which wasn't fun. I brought masks to protect our head and face while we worked outside. Summer days on the farm were humid and boiling hot, but during black fly season we were unable to wear short sleeves because black fly bites were painful. Those little buggers went straight for our blood. A few times, I got nauseous and lightheaded from them. Fortunately the season didn't last long.

My gut was still weak and I suffered from a lot of digestive problems, but the connection to growing our own food and nourishing ourselves was another piece to my health puzzle. Dennis King, was a wildlife biologist turned farmer who spent a long time building his soil. As a result, his vegetables were fantastic. In the garden, we grew a host of different vegetables and tomatoes inside a hoop house. We had access to King Hill Farm lamb, beef, mutton, chicken, duck and turkey. It was amazing to eat almost all of our food from the farm. Somewhere along the way I got rid of my vegetarian cookbooks and started reading Sally Fallon's cookbook, *Nourishing Traditions, The Cookbook that Challenges Politically Correct Nutrition and the Diet Dictocrats.* We started slow-cooking our pasture raised chicken and beef. The difference between pasture-raised food and conventional food became a visceral understanding.

We ate lunch with Dennis and Laura almost every day and because the work was physically demanding, we often settled down to a buffet of various food choices. One day, Dennis walked in for lunch and was shocked. "Holy shit " every day is Thanksgiving with you guys," he exclaimed. He was right, we definitely didn't hold back when it came to eating healthy food. For us, the physical demands of farming went hand in hand with eating like kings!

When Dennis worked on his tractor or walked with animals, or taught us specifics in the garden, he glowed. He had a way of blending into the landscape and with the animals as if he was an extension of them. That was his land; farming was clearly his calling. It was an extraordinary feeling working closely with another master. He talked frequently about a farmer in Virginia, Joel so and so. Dennis replicated the way Joel farmed with animals on pasture and moved daily. Being new to farming, we didn't recognize the name, but we sensed Dennis was inspired by this Joel guy. Several years later we realized Dennis was talking about Joel Salatin, our future mentor.

At King Hill Farm, we were introduced to human manure. The outside toilet at the main farmhouse consisted mainly of a bucket and sawdust. Once a week, we were responsible for cleaning it out. It took us some time to get on board with that primitive setting, but we did. And we learned the value of using our own waste as a resource. After the human manure was collected, it was composted in pasture and sat for two years. I appreciated how nothing went to waste on that farm.

After living in the city for so many years and buying fresh food at the farmers market, it was a revelation to see where it actually came from, how it took form, and what it needed to thrive. I loved being on the land working with the animals. When I worked in the garden I could feel the subtle energy of the plants as they extended their life.

Life was rich in a new way. Working in the elements day after day took away all false presumptions. I put my makeup away and started to welcome the earthy look and feeling that took its place. City habits quickly faded away. By the end of the day, we were filthy dirty and exhausted but deeply fulfilled. The lifestyle of farming grew on us.

At first I was terrified about butchering animals, but in time my uneasiness dissipated. It became like anything else: part of the job. We were feeding ourselves, making the farm money, and providing people with great food. We were all in it together. After awhile it seemed odd to me that we were so far removed from the natural cycle of death when we lived in the city. The animals lived great lives on King Hill Farm. We all made sure of that.

Even though I was tired and sometimes shaky, I absolutely loved what we were doing. We worked Monday through Friday 8:00 a.m. until 5:00 p.m. Saturday was market day so we started at 6:00 a.m. and finished by 2:00 p.m. The minute we got home from the market, I crawled into bed for a long nap. Sometimes I was so exhausted, I stayed there until Sunday morning. My body was restoring itself and my mind, too. I felt less and less vulnerable about my health, and Michael had time to think, grieve, and to let go. Life was simplified.

I enjoyed watching Michael, Dennis, and Laura build a hay shed with lumber acquired from the farm. Rain or sun they worked on that shed until it was finished. It was a project Dennis had wanted to do for a long time, and when it was finished he was deeply satisfied.

Dennis's wife, Jo, also lived with MCS. We shared a similar story. She was exposed to mold in their farmhouse when the greenhouse was attached. Like me, she was sensitive to everything: synthetic chemicals, fresh paint, cigarettes, laundry scents, perfume, cologne, bleach, hair dyes, etc. We spoke the same language, and neither one of us had to guard against each other's personal lifestyle choices like strong perfumes or detergents. Jo was as eager as me to find answers for MCS. Throughout the season, we helped each other when we had dips in our health. We were a good match.

I was still uncertain about the story of cancer playing out in my body. I didn't want to give it any attention, but the reality was I had to show up for annual checkups. That meant I had to fly back to L.A. from Maine to see Dr. Eilber at UCLA.

I took a very small charter plane out of Maine to a larger airport. That short flight was incredible. Below us, everywhere I looked I noticed small bodies of water and trees. So many trees. Maine is such a beautiful state. As soon as I got the news that all was well with my test, I hustled back to Maine, our new sanctuary.

We met like-minded people who were apprenticing with other great farmers in the area. Eric Franks and Jasmine Richardson ran a booth at the Farmers Market for Horsepower Farm. We gravitated to them, their love for farming and their gentle natures. Eventually they apprenticed with Elliot Coleman at his farm: Four Seasons. Back then Elliot and his wife were regular customers of King Hill Farm's grass fed beef, poultry and pork. We took a Sunday, our one day off, and visited their beautiful farm. His hoop houses were loaded with incredible vegetables. Life on the East Coast was a whole new world for us. We welcomed the change from the inside out.

Maine's winter season was long and cold. In May, we found ourselves planting garlic during a snowstorm. Summer comes and goes in a flash, and before you know it, the leaves are changing colors. At the end of our ten-month season Dennis and Jo invited us to stay, build a house on the land and manage their business. The opportunity was tempting, but Maine was too cold for too long for this California couple. Moving on from King Hill Farm was bittersweet for us. It was hard to walk away from our rich educational experience on the East Coast, but living in Maine permanently wasn't our next logical step.

Instead, we arranged for me to fly back out West to Santa Barbara to an interview for a caretaking job in The Santa Ynez Valley. Years ago, when we were newly married and lived in Topanga Canyon, we worked for a woman in the entertainment industry. She wanted to hire us again to take care of horses, dogs, and pigs on her new ranch while she lived in the Caribbean almost full-time. The interview was short but insightful. I really appreciated seeing the valley before deciding to move there, and I was amazed we camped all around Santa Ynez when we lived in Los Angeles but never explored the small peaceful town. There were already over 100 vineyards, with more on the way. Having access to local farms was now a priority to us and fortunately, the local food movement was also alive. Eventually we discovered a handful of small farmers nestled amongst horse ranches and vineyards. Although we would be returning to California, Michael and I knew moving to the valley would be another adventure. The ranch wasn't a farm, but it was a natural environment with a lot of privacy in a beautiful landscape. There was something interesting and different about the valley that we immediately appreciated.

Wine Country

After we left King Hill Farm in Maine we spent several weeks in Ohio visiting my family. During our short visit we stayed with my sister Chris and enjoyed quality time with her, my parents and the rest of my family. Although Brian, my brother, would never admit it, his lifestyle of drinking and drug usage finally caught up with him. He was super thin, his stomach constantly rumbled as if it was upset, and his face was red and puffy like a blowfish. Brian looked unhealthy and deficient. It wasn't the first time I was concerned about him. As a family we learned to accept his addictions, but we never gave up hope that one day he just might want a better life, perhaps even a sober life.

Several years had passed since my sister Amy died so naturally Chelsey and Blair's lives had taken on a routine and rhythm of their own. Chelsey was in grade school and growing up fast. Since Blair enjoyed cooking, during our visit we had dinner at their house a few times. Blair still traveled every month so my sister Chris, or my parents stayed with Chelsey when he was out of town. Other times she stayed with her next door neighbors. Spending time with my family was the perfect transition before heading back to the West Coast.

We arrived in Southern California during a very wet, unusual winter. A tremendous amount of flooding was occurring in January 2006. California needed water, but the rain was nonstop for two weeks. It was too much for the ground to absorb at one time. The coast was very green and beautiful, but mudslides were rampant and some of the consequences were devastating. In a small town near Santa Barbara, the damage was irreversible. Some families lost their homes and their lives.

The Santa Ynez Valley was new territory for us. The people who gravitated to the valley had an appetite for privacy, starry nights, and a slower-paced, small-town way of life. A lot of people came to Santa Ynez from L.A. to enjoy second homes.

The twenty-acre ranch we were responsible for was located in a gated community. There was a 300-square-foot guesthouse, newly remodeled, that became our home. I was relieved there were no traces of mold. The estate was very private and quiet, with a Spanish-style house that was under renovation.

Our new environment grew on us quickly. All over the property, lichen hung gently on various oak trees, giving the estate a mystical feeling. Blue oaks, live oaks, valley oaks: the trees were very old and magnificent. We came face to face with a variety of wildlife in the quiet gated community. Michael rescued a red-tailed hawk from the horses' water trough, and I stumbled upon an injured baby fawn. At night we had great horned owls, bats, coyotes, and bobcats to keep us company.

Miles, our dalmatian was reunited with some of his old buddies from our Topanga Canyon days. When we first arrived the dogs acted as if they remembered one another. I had Miles plus three additional dogs to walk, each one with its own affectionate personality. Miles of course became the alpha dog. The horses and pigs were easy to care for and provided continuous entertainment. After King Hill Farm, the caretaking job was a breeze. By spring of 2006 we had lived in the Santa Ynez Valley nearly three months, and every day we found something new to appreciate.

Loss

I was headed down south to see our holistic dentist in Tijuana, Mexico, when my sister Erin called with the news that our brother Brian had been found dead in his apartment. It was an unsettling and painful message to receive, but not entirely surprising. Michael and I had just visited with Brian after we left the farm in Maine. It was obvious to us then, his health was compromised. His body suffered from years of personal neglect.

Growing up, everyone was sort of empathetic to Brian because he was the only boy in the middle of seven sisters. At times we drove him crazy. In spite of all this, Brian was funny, generous, smart, intense, and fearless. He lived for good music and good times. Neil Young, Bob Dylan and the Beatles were just a few of his favorite musicians. Whenever Brian left the house I would go into his room without his permission and play his records. "Blackbird" and "Rocky Raccoon" by the Beatles were two songs he played over and over. I was too young to know what those songs were about, but like my big brother, I found them both irresistible.

It's hard to say at exactly what age he started getting high and drinking, but by the time he was twenty years old, he was deep into addiction. Many times, my parents tried to redirect his life. Like an intervention my father gathered him and all of his friends in our basement for a meeting. Dad recited all the reasons getting high and drinking were a waste of time, then he begged them to stop before it was too late. His words fell on deaf ears. Shortly after that meeting, Brian wrecked his mini-bike at the end of our street. I was outside playing when he walked up to the house with a bloody face. His injuries terrified me and I ran inside screaming for someone to help him. He suffered a concussion from that accident, and almost lost one of his eyes. Everyone assumed he was high at the time of the accident. The doctor wrapped his entire head in white bandages for a week. When he was feeling better we teased him because he looked like a mummy. He was a tough, brave and indomitable kid addicted to extremes.

I couldn't blame Brian for his overwhelming desire to feel good. In a way, I knew where he was coming from. Back then, life did indeed feel better with a little buzz, but his appetite for oblivion was borderline insane. Eventually his compulsion for alcohol and drugs destroyed his marriage and deeply affected the lives of his two sons in a negative way. At one point, he got busted for dealing drugs and went to prison for a short time. After his release, he started using and selling all over again, addiction had him pinned. It became too painful to watch my big brother continue to self-destruct, so I lost track of large portions of his life.

Although he'd never admit it, he drove drunk or high all the time. Many times he could have caused an accident and taken another person's life with his carelessness. It was a huge relief to all of us that he died at home. As it turns out, prior to his death, his ex-wife said he was sick for some time but refused to see a doctor. I think his fear of Western medicine stemmed from watching our sister Amy fade away in the hospital after her bone marrow transplant was unsuccessful. It's possible Brian knew he was sick and dying, but he decided to go it alone. After an autopsy, we were all shocked to learn he didn't have any alcohol or drugs in his system the day he died; instead, he went peacefully in his sleep. It was a miracle. My brother was forty-six years old when he died of complications from pneumonia in March 2005.

After my sister Amy died, Chelsey's dad continued to work as an entertainer for the Royal Caribbean Cruise Line. Because Blair's schedule required him to travel frequently, my parents or my sister Chris stayed with Chelsey when he was out of town. A few days before he was scheduled to leave with his new girlfriend for a January cruise in 2006, I felt a strong desire to connect with him. So I called Blair and left a lighthearted message wishing them both a safe trip to St. Thomas.

Less than a week later, our phone inside our small guesthouse in Santa Ynez rang before daybreak. Disoriented and half asleep, Michael motioned to me to pick it up. In between my sister Erin's cries, I heard something about Blair, a gunshot, and St. Thomas. I thought for sure I was having a bad dream. I tried catching my breath, fumbled out of bed, and asked my sister to repeat her message. When she did, the light inside me deflated, and I collapsed on our bathroom floor. Michael overheard me exclaiming, "My god, what about our little girl?" Chelsey's father was dead.

I was devastated and wanted to pull the phone cord out of the wall. It hadn't even been a year since we buried our brother Brian. Could we at least catch our breath before more bad news found us? I was tired of receiving those heartbreaking phone calls about dead family members. First Kim, then Amy, then Frank, then Brian, and now Blair. Hearing that kind of news before dawn left me feeling raw and helpless. Before I lost all my bearings, I quickly called my sister Chris, in Ohio, to get the details. As it turned out, after his performance on the cruise ship, Blair and his girlfriend checked into a Best Western Hotel on St. Thomas. Although they had a reservation, it wasn't on record, and the hotel was full. So the clerk sent them across the island to another Best Western. They checked in and then spent the day shopping and sightseeing.

When they returned to their room later that evening, they left their sliding glass door ajar, while Blair made his routine phone call to Chelsey before her bedtime. Shortly after they hung up, a young man appeared with a gun and demanded Blair's watch and money. When Blair walked towards him to offer both, the kid got nervous and shot him. It took more than twenty-five minutes for an ambulance to arrive at the scene, and by the time they did, Chelsey's dad was dead.

Cancer, fatal car accidents, pneumonia, old age: each had their reality, but murder carries a different weight. It took the air right out of my body, the color out of my face, and engulfed my entire spirit. Our hearts ached for Chelsey. It was January 2006 and her fourteenth birthday was the following week. Even though her dad traveled a lot, he always made it home to celebrate her special day.

My sister Chris is her guardian and the only aunt living in Ohio, so when Chelsey got home from school, she assumed the responsibility of telling her. Expecting her father to walk through the door any minute, she thought Chris was lying when she said her father was involved in an accident. I waited across the country in a dense fog of anguish for Chelsey to call me. When the phone rang, my heart sank. The first thing she said to me was, "I'm an orphan now." Words eluded me.

I was eager to get back to Ohio for Blair's funeral, but I waited until I felt capable of being fully present for Chelsey. My experience with death is that after a loved one passes, there's a brief window of time when this world and the hereafter are thin, almost transparent. It's a portal, a veil, a sacred interval of timelessness, and I knew it intimately. I couldn't eat, I could barely walk, and I had very little to say. I felt raw, like my heart was exposed. Michael knew firsthand the pain I was feeling. Already a man of few words, he let the power of silence restore me. He was one hundred percent present, open, and compassionate while I grieved. Our snug guesthouse got very quiet. Without him at my side, I'm not sure I could have faced another loss. This marked the fifth untimely death in our family. His presence buffered the agony.

I found it difficult to sleep, so in the middle of the night, I asked for something bigger to hold me, embrace me, make me a believer in life again. I felt the impulse to get on my knees and pray, I was desperate for direction. The following day I called my mentor and old friend, Gary David. I had introduced him to Chelsey when she visited us in California after her mom died. He knew how much my niece meant to me. It was hard for even him to believe the news about Blair. When I asked him for suggestions, his advice was straightforward and simple: "Hold onto your integrity."

Later in the week, after what the Jewish tradition calls "sitting Shiva", I felt my heart lift a little, so I bought a plane ticket to Ohio to bury another loved one. Fortunately our caretaking responsibilities were somewhat minimal that time of the year but since one of us needed to tend to the animals, Michael stayed behind.

I refused to wear the color black to Blair's funeral. Quite frankly, I was tired of burying family members and although I have deep respect for the process of grieving, I felt an urgency to embrace hope so I wore white. Nearly five hundred people attended Blair's funeral. His death was a shock to his immediate family and community. Everyone was despondent about losing Blair, but no one had the words to describe what they felt better than his daughter, Chelsey. When Chelsey got up to read a letter she wrote to her father, there wasn't a dry eye in the house. Afterwards the entire congregation stood in applause.

My dear father,

You were stolen from me, from all of us, in the most unfair of ways, and much too soon. We should have spent years and years more together. Our house still stands, the world still turns, but my life will be forever altered and forever incomplete without your gentle, unwavering love. You taught me and everyone around you so much, and you could brighten one's day with only a few words.

The tears I've shed are countless. You were the strength in my life, the comfort, the warmth, the love; you were the guidance, the support, and I always did my best to make you proud, and I still will. For you made me proud every day, and you still do.

You were the most gentle and thoughtful of men. Why you? Why us? What will I ever do without you, Daddy? It is so hard for me to accept that from this trip, you'll never return, that you'll never again hold me in your arms, never again laugh with me, never again tell me you love me.

As we lay you to rest, we remember all the countless precious memories we all shared with you, or else we remember what a hilarious, cheering, kind man you were. I promise you that you'll never be forgotten by anyone who knew you.

As for me, I'll remember you as the best father I ever could have asked for. My eternal wish is that we could have had more time on earth together, but at the same time, I look forward to someday coming home to your embrace once more.

I love you, I love you, I love you and I know you will help me, and all of those who you loved, pull through this.

After Blair's funeral I was exhausted and when I returned home to our caretaking job in Santa Ynez I nearly collapsed into Michael's arms at the airport. As we pulled into the gated community and drove toward our guesthouse, I was overcome by the beauty and private, quiet setting we inhabited. It felt good to be home. Once again the generous embrace of nature mended my weary heart. Getting back into the rhythm of everyday responsibilities, massage clients and tending to the animals, took a few days but eventually those distractions became part of my healing process.

With both parents dead, there was a lot of confusion about Chelsey's future. Would she come to California and live with Michael and me? Would she stay with my parents and my sister? What environment was best for her? My sister Chris had a very full life on the other side of town, but she loved her niece as much as the rest of us, and being the kind-spirited person she is, she put her life on hold and moved into Chelsey's home so that she could finish the school year. Nick and Andrew, Chris's two sons, pitched in when Chris went to work.

It may have seemed to some people that I had no business getting involved with the details of Chelsey's future, but there was no room for that opinion in my mind. I'd made a promise to my sister Amy that I would do whatever I could for her daughter, and I had every intention of keeping my word. After experiencing so much loss, I knew Chelsey's life could easily take a turn for the worst, and I refused to stand back and watch her world fall apart even more. Several months after Blair's funeral, there were some lingering details that needed attention, so I returned to Ohio and stayed with Chelsey.

The door to her dad's room was barricaded, and no one was allowed to enter without her permission. Next to the bed was Blair's unpacked suitcase from his last cruise. My sister Chris and I thought it was time for closure. I asked Chelsey if she would join me unpacking her dad's suitcase, she agreed. One by one we removed his personal things. First his robe, then his work shirts, a bottle of Tylenol, his toothbrush. Neither one of us could talk; tears clouded our vision. I felt I should be strong for Chelsey, so I kept my grief in check. But what I wanted to do was lie down on Amy and Blair's bedroom floor and wail. Their absence from that house was absolutely unbearable. Photos from the past hung on every wall. It was like being in a haunted house. I couldn't feel the promise of Chelsey's future anywhere. By the time Blair's suitcase was empty, we both felt relieved. The door to her dad's room remained open from that point on.

It was during that trip back to Ohio when I understood the words of wisdom from my mentor Gary David. Those words, "hold onto your integrity," were a clear message that it was impossible for me to save Chelsey from the pain of her losses. No matter how much I wanted to, I couldn't bring her parents back.

Eventually Chelsey moved in with my sister and my parents on the other side of town in Cincinnati. The best thing that happened for her in that move was that she changed schools and enrolled in the School for Creative and Performing Arts. It was an entirely new world for her. She found refuge in the arts. The irony was that it's the school her father had hoped she might one day attend.

"I'm standing with a group of people around a fire pit, we're part of a ritualistic ceremony. A woman wearing a dark mask dances around the ring of fire, she approaches each one of us, when she gets to me she looks into my eyes and forewarns me about death."

I had that dream two weeks before Blair left for his final cruise, but I failed to make the connection to him and the dream until two weeks after he was murdered. A friend suggested the woman in the dream was Kali, the hindu Goddess of life, death and rebirth. Perhaps she was right.

My Aunt Jo lived in Cleveland and was ecstatic about our move to Virginia. She was convinced it would be a positive transition for us and she welcomed us living closer to her. In the fall of 2010 right before we left the Santa Ynez Valley, Aunt Jo shared the following dream with me.

"I'm flying through the Grand Canyon; it's magnificent all around me. I fly down and down and down deeper into the canyon. I see the ridges; the colors. It's a wonderful feeling. I feel the air, the breeze, the speed of the wind; the breeze goes through my panties. The force of the air and speed on my body is delicious. Then I hear a deep voice say, 'It's time.' No, not yet, this feels so good. 'Soon' I wake up."

As I listened to Aunt Jo I knew the dream was preparing both of us for her death. I didn't voice my feelings to her, because I didn't want to frighten her, but I knew her dream was a premonition.

When we drove across the country form California to Virginia, she lived vicariously through us. I phoned her each time we entered a new state and described our travels, where we were staying, what we were eating, what the weather was like, and how long before our next state. I could feel her excitement through the phone. But, once we arrived at Buxton Farm her health quickly started to deteriorate. She had respiratory challenges and was living with oxygen full-time. Her anxiety attacks increased and she had spells where she was unable to catch her breath. She was seeing more and more of the emergency room. Doctors gave her one pill after another; she struggled with a variety of side effects and no lasting solutions.

Jo was my father's sister, but not by blood. My father was adopted. I enjoyed the stories she shared about my dad's side of the family, things my father never revealed. Less than two months after we moved to Buxton Farm, Jo went into the hospital in Cleveland, Ohio. We talked on the phone every day; she didn't like being there. During our phone conversations I could tell she was very weak and frustrated. After a few days, our conversations grew shorter, and her sentences were no longer making sense. When she went into intensive care, I felt an urge to get to her as soon as possible.

The following day Michael and I were listening to Garrison Keillor's "Prairie Home Companion" radio show and preparing dinner when a warm flush of energy filled my whole body. I felt the impulse to get very still, so I went upstairs and laid down. Memories of Aunt Jo flooded my mind. I was deep in meditation when Michael came up to check on me. My heart was very heavy. Together, we reflected on Aunt Jo's life. A few hours later we received a message that Aunt Jo died. I wasn't with her physically when she passed, but I was with her in spirit, and even though I was pleased she was no longer in the hospital suffering, I missed her funny jokes, interesting stories, and eagerness for life.

Fortunately, the cows had already gone back to Polyface for winter, so Michael and I drove to Cleveland to close up Jo's personal affairs. We'd lived on the East Coast just three months and so appreciated being free and available to deal with the details of her transition. In a way, it seemed she waited for us to get across the country.

I've never been drawn to Cleveland, and being there without Jo felt awkward to me. I was glad Michael was with me. It took a few days to settle Auntie Jo's personal affairs. At her request, we didn't have a funeral but instead celebrated her long life. Her good friends, former co-workers and clients, and AA friends attended. We lit a candle and passed it, and each of us shared a story about Aunt Jo. She would have been pleased because everyone was laughing. We brought her ashes back to Buxton in a Chock Full o'Nuts coffee canister. The guy at the funeral parlor looked at me like I was "nuts" when I told him her final wish was to be put in a Chock Full o'Nuts canister. In fact, she saved that can under her kitchen sink for years just for that purpose. It was waiting for us when we cleared out her apartment. I left her ashes in that canister until I felt compelled to cast them one day on a new moon.

There was a strange routine in our lives with death. Every time, within a few months of settling into a new home, someone near and dear to us passed on. It's a pattern I can track all the way back to my initial move to California, when my sister Kim died three months later. I may never understand the significance of our new beginnings being somehow linked to endings for loved ones, but I do know that every time someone I love dies, the impulse within me to embrace life deepens.

A Beast and A Dog

We turned our caretaking position and our new life in Santa Ynez into a great opportunity. The area was filled with all sorts of interesting people, and getting to know some of them made it feel more like home to us. We enjoyed group hikes at The Sedgwick Reserve, as well as live music at Tales from the Tavern and Live Oak Music Festival. We also attended a variety of events just over the mountain in Santa Barbara, so we spent a fair amount of time driving Highway 154 from Santa Ynez to Santa Barbara. That busy thoroughfare was the quickest route to Santa Barbara from our guest house. It's a beautiful drive, and if driven too fast, can be deadly.

One evening we were headed back to Santa Ynez after attending a lecture at UCSB. As we came around a tight bend, we thought there was a dead body lying on the side of the road. Once we got closer, we realized it was a dead bear. It was hard to believe. Seeing bears so close to the road in that part of the country was rare. Michael pulled over, we got out of the car, and within minutes several other people joined us. The bear was enormous. I bent down to get close to him. He was recently hit, so his body was still warm. Standing above that fantastic beast, we realized there was no way he was hit by a car, his large frame surely would have caused serious damage to an automobile. It must have been a fast-driving semi truck. There was hardly any blood. We were hopeful it was a pain-free fast death. Nonetheless, it was a struggle to witness firsthand the death of that gorgeous creature. Even though we were in close proximity to brown bears when we visited Katmai National Park in Alaska, that was nothing compared to standing there holding the paws of that dead bear and touching his staggeringly gorgeous face.

Almost every morning I took our sweet dalmatian, Miles, along with the three other dogs from our caretaking job on long walks before breakfast. Bluebell, Chocolate and Zoey weren't in great shape so they were often somewhat behind Miles and me, but we enjoyed their company anyway. One morning we were headed back to our guesthouse when Miles suddenly collapsed in our driveway. His behavior seemed to come out of nowhere. He hadn't shown any signs of illness until that moment. The day before, he was leading the way on our daily walk with his buddies. He was fifteen years old, and until that day, his health was outstanding. When he was a puppy, he had seizures, so we took him to an alternative vet in Los Angeles, and she recommended a raw meat and vegetable diet instead of dog food. After a week on the diet, the seizures stopped and from that point forward, we steamed vegetables for him every day and fed him a pound of raw meat. Sometimes we included cooked white or brown rice. The diet made him super strong and fueled his longevity.

A few days after his first collapse, he stumbled over again, so I took him to the vet. X-rays showed a large sarcoma tumor on his spleen. I was shocked when the vet said it was a "sarcoma;" it was the same name they used to describe the tumor in my leg. The thought of losing Miles brought tremendous heartache. His companionship over the years had been the center of our lives. The three of us were a tight knit family and up until this point he seemed almost invincible, as if he would live with us forever. But we weren't about to bombard his body with invasive treatments to keep him alive for us, so we made a decision to make the end of his life as pain-free as possible. The vet's recommendation was to take him home, enjoy the weekend with him, then put him to sleep on Monday. I barely escaped that office in one piece. Driving home sobbing, Miles sensed something wasn't right.

That weekend Miles didn't let me or Michael out of his sight. We had three magical days together. We were so appreciative of the small window of time we had for closure with Miles. On Monday morning, Michael went up the hillside on the property we were caretaking and dug a hole. Throughout the day we started telling Miles goodbye. Friends called to give their support, and Miles whimpered in the background when I told them what was happening. His behavior amazed me; it was as if he knew what I was telling them.

Living in horse country, we had the option of hiring a mobile vet to come to our guesthouse to put him down. We held Miles closely while the vet injected him. When life left his body, the vet gave us our privacy. I was so pleased Miles remained at home for his transition, but the grief was impossible for us to contain. Somehow Michael found the strength to put Miles over his shoulder and carry him up the hill. At the top, I had to peel myself away from Miles' dead body.

The next few days were like living on another planet. Miles was no longer there to greet us every morning; walks with his buddies felt vacant. His protective bark when someone pulled up to the property was gone. The companionship, protection, happiness, and unconditional love he gave us was remarkable. I knew it would be years before we'd choose to get another dog.

Expeditions

In 2002, after surgery and treatment for cancer, I couldn't postpone my desire to get back into nature any longer, it's where I feel my best. My scalded leg from treatment healed and I was eager to put a bathing suit on and swim again. For years, I had read about the lush landscapes and tranquil atmosphere Hawaii offered. Many times I wondered if we would enjoy living in that kind of environment. I knew we would never know until we visited, so Kauai was our next destination.

In Kauai we explored remote beaches, exquisite waterfalls, and Waimea Canyon State Park. Right away we noticed the pace of the island was slower than Los Angeles. We immediately appreciated the contrasting environment. Although we weren't accustomed to the green landscapes or the afternoon rain showers, we took advantage of both. We swam every morning and every afternoon. The ocean was immensely healing. Moving my legs in the water was incredibly gratifying. My left leg now felt different from my right leg, but eventually I acclimated to the distinct variances between the two. The surgery left a large scar on the back of my thigh, and every time I looked at it in the mirror, I felt short-changed, as if the scar belonged on someone else's body. The silver lining on that vacation was that I had no complaints. I could walk, swim, and travel like a normal person. Getting away was the perfect re-entry into life for me. I understood why Hawaii was considered paradise, and I was so pleased I was alive to experience it.

There's something about traveling that frees up restless spirits. In the early days of our marriage Michael and I spent a lot of time camping in the back country of Big Sur, California and other beautiful hiking spots across the state. Getting out of the city to explore in nature always restored us but we were eager to take a trip out of the country together. Without children, we had the freedom to go almost anywhere we wished. One place everyone raved about was Indonesia. Friends spoke highly of the culture and beautiful landscape. We were ready for a pilgrimage outside of the U.S. We made the long journey there in June 1999.

We took advantage of the services the Balinese offered and soaked in hot herbal baths, relaxed with deep tissue massages, and explored ancient temples. The Balinese live humble but opulent lives; even their children seemed different to us. They seemed much older than their years and had a fearlessness about them. The scenery was breathtaking and the people were rich in ways some Americans might not be able to comprehend. Material possessions simply weren't a priority to them. There was ritual to everything the Balinese people did. Dancing, cooking, working, playing— there was a reverence in all their daily routines. We found their presence very friendly and when they spoke, they looked us in the eye.

Michael chose a spot on the beach for us to visit outside of Bali called Ahmed. We hired a driver and drove three hours out to the countryside. It was a long and bumpy ride filled with fantastic landscapes. We discovered a Balinese family who owned a hotel in Ahmed called "Good Karma." They rented bungalows on the beach for eight dollars a night and offered home cooked meals in their small restaurant. The environment was laid back and friendly. Ocean views were stunning. Every morning we went for a long swim. Good Karma was paradise. In the distance the sounds of drumming and singing echoed. Villagers informed us a child was born and the families were celebrating new life. It was heartwarming to hear their beautiful commemoration.

We were committed to avoiding foods in Bali that might cause food poisoning, so in addition to being conscious about our food choices, we also took homeopathic remedies and probiotics with us and ate them with our meals. Mostly, we ate rice, broths and veggies. Then we celebrated our spectacular journey with one final lunch before our long flight back to the U.S. It was hot out the day of our departure and without thinking I ordered a lasse, a milk drink similar to a light yogurt smoothie. Less than a few hours later I was bent over with excruciating stomach pain followed with fever and diarrhea. On our long flight home I was dehydrated and miserable. Back in the States I spent months trying everything I could to eradicate a parasite from my body. I fasted, took herbs, ate specific foods and I lost a lot of weight. Eliminating that parasite became a systemic problem that contributed to my health challenges. It was a tough way to end a fantastic journey and felt a bit more like, "bad karma," rather than good karma.

Nature has a soothing way; it's powerful medicine. Not long after my sister Amy's death in 1998, I was eager to get out of the city and explore new horizons. I wanted to explore the "last frontier." After watching a nature program, Michael and I decided to visit Katmai National Park and Preserve in Alaska. Katmai is located in the Valley of Ten Thousand Smokes and is known for its pristine waterways, abundant fish, remote wilderness and brown bears. It's one of the most heavily visited bear-viewing areas in the world, and requires a bit of navigating to find. We flew to Anchorage, then boarded two additional charter planes until we landed in the breathtaking valley. The unspoiled air quality was awesome. The park was very busy with tourists arriving and leaving on charter flights all day. It's a haven for wildlife photographers. Many tourists came only for the day, took photos, ate lunch and left, but we decided to camp out for four nights.

Tour guides escorted visitors through the woods to the different viewing platforms along the Brooks River, where bears congregated at Brooks Falls to feed on sockeye salmon. As a group, we'd walk slowly through the brush with our hands up in the air softly saying, "hey bear, hey bear." On every side of us, bears foraged for their next meal. It was exhilarating to witness. It was also a bit of an adrenaline rush and amazing to be within reach of these impressive beasts. The salmon running in the river worked so hard to move upstream, only to be swallowed whole by the bears. The bears caught them with proficiency, and devoured them in seconds. The river was clear, cold and loaded with fresh fish, and since there was a pecking order sometimes bears would fight over salmon.

The rugged scenery was riveting. We were surrounded by incredible endless horizons. On clear nights, colors of the rainbow radiated against the mountainside. Daylight was almost continuous. Midnight felt like 8:00 p.m. Sometimes it was impossible to sleep.

It was considered normal to be walking on the beach within feet of a brown bear. They roamed all around us. We camped for several nights in the primitive campground where bears could walk right through any time. We secured our food in a locked container with an electric fence surrounding it. Although the bears seemed calm and disinterested in us, night time was a little unnerving.

After a few days in the pristine environment, I felt eager to move on. My change of heart occurred after watching a very hungry mom and her three cubs struggle to find food. Their territory was closer to the lodge, a very busy area with charter flights coming and going all day. The planes and the people were a distraction. Clearly she was having a hard time foraging with so many people around her. She was super thin and stressed. After watching her compete with tourist for space, it became apparent to me that we were nothing more than an interference. Instead of being in awe of Katmai, I felt remorse for intruding on the brown bears in their home. In the end it seemed to me they were being exploited. It was true that traveling to remote places to bask in nature gave us tremendous amounts of joy, but by the time our charter flight arrived to pick us up, I concluded that some places are better left untouched.

We traveled on to Valdez, "Alaska's Little Switzerland," where the mountains meet the sea. At Prince William Sound, we took a cruise out to the glaciers where we watched humpback whales. It was riveting. Once again, we savored the incredible crisp air, filled our bellies with a variety of delicious fresh seafood; the best we have ever tasted! Just outside of Valdez, we camped for the evening. The evening air was cool and filled with mosquitoes, but the quiet night was exactly what we needed.

Next, we traveled out to the McCarthy-Kennicott area located near Wrangell-St. Elias National Park and Preserve. Without four wheel drive in our rental car it was a bit of a hike across rugged terrain. We rented the last private room at a small hostel. When we walked into the kitchen a very pungent smell quickly caught our attention. The owner confessed he prepared bear meat the night before our arrival. Troublesome bears were extinguished, but instead of shooting problematic bears and discarding them into the river like his neighbors, he ate them and tanned the hide for his personal use. We were impressed with his resourcefulness.

The area was an old mining town with less than fifty full-time residents, and the hiking was magnificent. It took a certain kind of character to settle down in a lifestyle that rugged. We lingered for several days in the exquisite quiet setting before heading back to Los Angeles. Traveling provided us with new insights and with every trip we took, we got closer and closer to creating a life outside of Los Angeles.

When we lived in Maine we were introduced to WWOOF, Worldwide Opportunities on Organic Farms, a nonprofit organization connecting farmers to volunteers worldwide. Michael thought WWOOFing through Italy would be educational and more intimate than staying in standard hotel rooms, so in Spring of 2005 we joined WWOOF ITALY and chose a few farms that sparked our interest. The agreement between volunteers and farmers was that we worked five hours a day in exchange for room and board.

The first family we chose to visit was in Tuscany. Their estate was small with superb views of vineyards below. In some ways it reminded us of wine country in Santa Ynez, where we lived. The owner was practicing Permaculture principles, which was totally new to us. She had a large kitchen garden, fruit trees, and chickens. Little did we know that brief introduction to permaculture would turn into something much more personal to us when we returned to the States. Her and her daughter lived in the guesthouse and tourist rented the main house; it was spacious and elegant with a tremendous amount of history.

It was early spring, and the air was revitalizing. The main house needed organizing, cleaning, and some yard work. We moved large rocks from the garden into the pond. Some of the rocks were enormous, so Michael and I carefully lifted one after another together so that we didn't strain or injure our backs. We did a lot of heavy lifting our first day on that homestead. By early afternoon, I would lie down in the yard and take a short nap. Evening meals we gathered together and shared life experiences, ideas, spiritual yearnings and great conversation. The family had a very strong aversion to material possessions. After living with simplicity most of our lives, Michael and I could relate. In winter they traveled to Ecuador where they lived in an intentional community and practiced meditation. Their unpretentious lifestyle made an impression on us.

Orvietto in Umbria wasn't originally on our list of places to visit, but when the family in Tuscany recommended we check out the mystical town, we took their advice. Located on top of a tufa, a large piece of volcanic stone, the dramatic city is unique. We were captivated by the pedestrian-friendly cobblestone streets, the Duomo cathedral, small shops, and restaurants. Views from the city were outstanding. There is a labyrinth of underground galleries, quarries, cellars, stairs and unexpected passageways that piqued our curiosity, but our time was limited. I knew if we ever had the opportunity to return to Italy, that sweet town would be one destination we'd spend more time exploring. It's gorgeous. We enjoyed a light but fantastic lunch before our journey to Bologna, our next destination.

We were in seventh heaven with the extensive train system throughout Europe. We would be sightseeing in Rome, and two hours later enjoying lunch in Tuscany. It was my second time visiting Rome, and I thrived in that city.

Michael thought we'd enjoy working on a small lavender farm, so we traveled high up into the mountains outside of Bologna to a small village. An extended Italian family lived together in a restored beautiful villa, and the daughter had turned the land into a lavender business. Together they were building her dream. The views from the lavender farm and the secluded village were exceptional. Snowcapped mountains surrounded us. Her Italian mother was an authentic cook and spoiled us with homemade pasta dishes, desserts, and the best chestnut cake I've ever tasted in my life! We felt at home with our host family and their affectionate children and grandchildren. Five hours a day, we weeded the lavender field. The weather was cool and the air at that elevation was supreme. While we worked we listened to the rare song of a cuckoo bird, a distinct and incredible sound that captivated us.

During our time off, we walked into the aging village and explored medieval structures. The terrain was rugged but families raised sheep, goats, and chickens on the steep ridges regardless. Kitchen gardens extended from family villas to curvy hillsides. I noticed older women working with goats and chickens in their gardens, and was inspired by their age and agility.

The quality of the lavender oil the family made was supreme. It was a wholesome product made without any chemicals, and it smelled divine. Before we left, I bought several bottles for friends and family. I could hardly wait to do massage again and use it on future clients. At the end of our commitment, it was hard to leave the humble family and their spectacular mountain oasis, but our next family and new region awaited us.

Driving down from the mountain to the train station with our hearts full, we set out for our next adventure, working on a straw bale house in Venetto, Italy. The owner was an incredibly interesting gay man with several children. It was an amicable separation, so the children were being raised by both parents despite their divorce. I was impressed with how they lived and worked out their differences. We felt welcomed by all of them.

Michael and I cleaned up the inside of the straw bale house, dusted, swept, cleaned windows, and worked outside in the kitchen garden. In the afternoons, we collected milk from a small dairy farmer down the road. The family was especially open-minded and curious about life in the States, so we enjoyed sharing stories with them. Venetto is agriculturally oriented, with very little other culture. It was another part of the country we appreciated seeing.

We walked off the train at our next stop and I thought we were in the middle of a movie set. The colors, energy, water, artistic ambience, the canals: Venice is a masterpiece. It seemed surreal, imaginary. What a dream to be in a city without automobiles. With no cars to dodge, we navigated our way through the beautiful romantic city at our own pace. The winding canals and narrow streets were fun to get lost in. The architecture is superb. Musicians played in front of churches, and photographers and tourists gather at Piazza San Marco. Coffee shops were filled with espresso lovers, and even though drinking caffeine wasn't a habit of ours, we stopped inside just to get a hit of the strong java aromas while grabbing a pastry to share. Venice is an intense and beautiful place but as unique as it was, I couldn't see living there. A heavy footprint of tourism left us slightly overwhelmed. I could see why some of the locals were distraught about the lack of privacy. In fact, after a few days we needed a little more breathing room ourselves, so we took the train back to Rome and decompressed before returning to the States.

I was so pleased Michael created an interesting trip through WWOOFing for us. It was a much more expansive and interesting way to get a feel for another country. We returned to California totally inspired, with a few new intentions for our future, and a handful of new recipes!

The Mystery of Illness

Our caretaking commitment in the gated community was for one year. As we came closer to that job ending, leaving it was a mixed bag for us. We would miss the peaceful private setting and the sweet animals, but we intended to move closer to Santa Barbara. By this time Michael was teaching "at risk" kids part-time in Santa Barbara, and I was working part-time at a small school and doing massage. We found a house halfway between both worlds on top of the mountain on San Marcos Pass Road. After seeing the rental and meeting Nina, our potential roommate, we thought for sure moving closer to Santa Barbara was our next step. Nina had a passion for nature, long hikes, animals, teaching children, camping, politics and reading. We shared a lot of the same interests. She had lived on the property for several years and loved it. The house had a separate entrance for us and a private bath, the kitchen and living space were shared. In the beginning it felt like a win-win.

Shortly after we moved in, I started getting migraines if I was inside the house for long periods of time. Then came brain fog, insomnia, and body aches. When Michael started to get headaches, too, we knew something wasn't right. The symptoms were too severe for us to ignore, so we investigated the situation. As it turned out, there was an old water leak in the house; mold was present. My body reacted to the point where I could no longer be inside without being uncomfortable, so I put our tent up and slept outside in the yard. With winter and cold weather just around the corner, it was impossible for us to stay, so we moved back down the mountain to the Santa Ynez Valley into a small apartment at the back of a woman's house. She had goats, horses, chickens, and a garden in her backyard. Her homestead was sweet and inviting. Our plan to get closer to Santa Barbara was abandoned.

Not long after moving out of Nina's house, I had to quit both of my part-time jobs. The same symptoms I felt in Nina's house were activated in the school where I worked. I started to feel like every place I entered had mold hidden somewhere. When the studio where I did massage decided to relocate, they painted the new space without low VOC paints and as soon as I walked through the door, I got a migraine. By this time, I was very frustrated with my body's inability to process everyday environmental exposures, and wondered if unconscious beliefs were compromising my immunity. I felt strongly that learning more about the factors influencing my immune system would help alleviate the reactions I had to chemicals. My deepest desire was to live free of MCS, so I continued to seek answers.

Fortunately, Santa Barbara has a host of wonderful healers, and after some inquiry, a few people came highly recommended to me. The first person I went to was a Jungian analyst. She suggested Carl Jung's book, *Memories, Dreams and Reflections.* She was an incredibly gifted therapist with excellent discernment. I was unable to sit inside her office because the strong smell of her beautiful italian leather furniture gave me a migraine, so I sat outside on her small patio while she sat inside the doorway. In Santa Barbara, we rarely had to deal with inclement weather conditions.

My intention with the analysis was to bring unconscious self limiting patterns into conscious awareness. I wanted to know if I unconsciously contributed to my suppressed immune system. In addition, I hoped to feel less vulnerable about my physical limitations related to MCS. Being unable to live and work where ever I wished created constant challenges; I was tired of living like a canary in a coal mine.

I had recorded my dreams for many years, so having an analyst to finally review them with me was terribly exciting. I knew the power of dreams and their ability to open doors into healing. The therapist was remarkable when it came to analyzing the powerful imagery in my dreams and extracting the meanings. Her insights were very compelling. Many times I didn't want the appointment to end! I took notes during our sessions and in between sessions reflected on our discoveries. Becoming familiar with the symbolism and significance of my recurring dreams was enlightening.

The sessions were extremely powerful and profound, and they weren't cheap. I did the best I could committing to them on a regular basis. In the end, the analysis took me to new levels of insight and helped me understand I wasn't responsible for the number of tragic untimely deaths in my family. My awareness expanded as a result of analysis and my ego strengthened, but despite a sincere intention to be free of MCS, I remained chemically sensitive.

In addition to analysis, I also saw a Chinese acupuncturist and herbalist. I had heard and known of people so sensitive to the environment and electromagnetic frequencies that they're only recourse is to live secluded on a mountaintop. Living a hermetic life had no appeal at all to me, but at times it seemed as if I was headed in that direction because MCS symptoms kept increasing.

I was relieved when the acupuncturist reassured me I didn't need to live in a state of vigilance regarding my immune system. In fact, he encouraged me to eliminate the belief that my body was incapable of handling exposures to toxins. Instead, his advice was to focus on building up the immune system. It wasn't like I had never heard these words before. Since my health challenges began, I had seen or tried a number of alternative modalities or practitioners; acupuncturist, holistic dentist, psychotherapist, homeopaths, chiropractors, yoga clases, kinesiologist, rolfers, nutritionist, naturopaths, hands-on healers, astrologers, bodyworkers, Ayurvedic medicine, I even saw a few psychics and had several sessions of biofeedback. It's true that every one of them helped me along the way, but none of them yet held the cure for MCS. The Chinese herbs strengthened my constitution, but they didn't stop my body from reacting with symptoms of MCS. Nonetheless, I remained determined to discover what blocked me from being well.

Another person I discovered in Santa Barbara was an incredibly strong and vibrant massage therapist who combined his knowledge of Naturopathic studies with bodywork. He is a gifted healer and has more stamina than most people half his age. I was blown away by his strength and massage techniques. He knew every acupressure point in my body. I'm certain the increase in lymphatic flow during his massages contributed to my overall feeling of improved health afterwards. One simple recommendation he suggested was to soak in epsom salt baths after each massage. He emphasized using the entire four pound box at one time and soaking in hot water for at least twenty minutes. The combination of deep massage, hot water and magnesium was exhilarating. I felt stress free after those baths and from that point forward they became a weekly ritual of mine. I always looked forward to those massage appointments, and I couldn't help but translate some of his unique massage techniques into my own practice as a bodyworker.

"Michael and me Los Angeles, California 2006"
(Photo by Jean Pierre)

Permaculture

Despite the Santa Ynez Valley being dominated by vineyards, in between the large estates are incredible small farmers growing vibrant food. These farms are vital to the community. Shopping at the Solvang farmers market every week gave me an opportunity not only to support local farmers, but also to get to know them. I met a woman with a small family farm who needed help weeding, organizing, sowing, and harvesting. I joined her on her farm on a part-time basis, and I was back in my element working with the soil, planting new life. She invited me to attend a lecture and book signing in Santa Barbara featuring Michael Abelman, an organic farmer and author of *Fields of Plenty, a Farmer's Journey of Real Food and the People Who Grow It*. I bought Abelman's book and read it within a week. Founder of The Center for Urban Agriculture in Santa Barbara California, Abelman is another person who inspired my desire to grow food.

In the high season I arrived at the small family farm just after dawn, when there was still a cool breeze in the valley, and I worked until lunch. Working outside in Santa Ynez was intense in summertime, but it was exactly where I wanted to be, so I learned how to pace myself in the heat. Often I would return home after lunch exhausted. I'd take a nap and then prepare for massage clients.

When the opportunity came to move from our very small apartment to a cottage on one acre in Los Olivos, we were thrilled. Downtown Los Olivos is a small wine-tasting town with a few restaurants, one of which Michael worked at as a waiter. The location was perfect. We rented the house from a new friend who owned the land for many years. Within no time at all, we became good friends with our neighbor across the street. Shelley and I shared a lot of common interests. She was an incredible gardener, had a passion for eating well, enjoyed hiking, and was interested in organizing events for the community. Together with Katherine and Maria, two other friends, we started The Santa Ynez Film Group. We brought progressive films about food and humanitarian issues to our local Rotary Club.

Around the same time, I insisted on improving my stamina so I started hiking in the back country with our previous roommate and friend, Nina. On one of those hikes, Nina introduced me to her friend, Margie Bushman, an educator with a deep passion for the principles of permaculture. Margie took her first Permaculture Design Course (PDC) with Bill Mollison in Ojai, California, and it changed her life. Since then her heart has been anchored in sustainability, she is truly a grassroots advisor. I appreciated her library of knowledge about sustainability. She started The Santa Barbara Permaculture Network with her good friend and colleague, Wesley Roe. Margie and Wes sponsored educational events on sustainability and brought fantastic speakers to the Coast. I attended as many of the workshops as possible. Paul Stamets, Gunter Pauli, Woody Tasch, Elaine Ingham, Art Ludwig, Brock Doleman, Brad Lancaster, Mark Lakeman, Toby Hemengwey, and many, many more.

I also had the privilege to hear Indian environmental activist and author, Vandana Shiva, as well as Kenyan environmentalist and political activist, Wangari Maathai, speak at UCSB. They were both committed to bringing awareness about the benefits of growing food and planting trees. I felt their passion and their devotion not only for the environment but for humanity too. Their passionate messages amplified my desire and interest in sustainable principles. I was in awe of their commitments.

When a new massage client passed onto me Michael Pollan's book, *The Omnivore's Dilemma, A Natural History of Four Meals,* I couldn't put it down. After reading about Joel Salatin and Polyface Farms, his family farm in Swoope Virginia, I felt inspired to learn more about growing food and farming on a larger scale. Another friend, recommended Barbara Kingsolver's book, *Animal, Vegetable, Miracle, A Year of Food Life.* I read it and became fascinated with the idea of eating only local food. I was also intrigued by Kingsolvers' decision to leave Arizona and move to Virginia to farm. Perhaps it was my Midwestern roots, but there were definitely times when I considered moving to a region with seasons again, and where water was more abundant.

When Margie encouraged me to sign up for a PDC with Geoff Lawton and Darren Doherty at Quail Springs Permaculture Farm in Ventura, California, I did! I assumed permaculture might expand my knowledge, but I had no idea it would dramatically change the way I perceived the world and my part in it.

The PDC was spread out over fourteen days. It was the very early stages of Quail Springs, and so the setting was quite rustic. We pitched tents across the landscape and started the morning with yoga, a quick dip in the pond, and a great breakfast. I admired the residents at Quail Springs because they were deeply committed to the land. Their ability to thrive despite the extreme atmosphere, amazed me. The climate in New Cuyama Valley was very intense. Mornings were mild and comfortable, but by mid-afternoon, heat combined with swift winds swept through the canyon. We took long siestas in the afternoon because it was too hot to hold class.

Geoff Lawton and Darren Doherty, instructors from Australia, were very passionate about Permaculture principles and their teaching styles were like night and day. Darren had extensive experience in Permaculture project design, Keyline design, and retrofitting broad-acre agricultural systems. He is a fantastic, lighthearted teacher with a great sense of humor. He made classes fun, interesting and easy to grasp. Lisa, his wife, and their three children traveled with him and homeschooled the kids. I was impressed with their lifestyle.

Geoff is a very methodical, serious teacher with a heart of gold. I liked the variance of having both of them as translators of my first design course. It was so exciting to see the number of gardens and sustainable sights Geoff created. His portfolio of work is boundless. He consulted with groups, communities, individuals, and governments all over the world. Being in class with him, I got a sense of his deep commitment to sustainability, as well as his sincere intention to pass onto others the profound, yet simplistic fundamentals of efficient design. His devotion to making the world a better place by simply starting a garden prompted my own desires to grow food.

My world was forever changed after that fourteen-day design course. As soon as it was over, I went home and got busy building our first garden. Michael and Brooks, the landowner, were both very supportive of my desire to start a garden. The first thing we did was take out our driveway and put raised beds in for vegetables. Then, Brooks dug a small pond with his tractor. The pond brought incredible wildlife. We watched beautiful white or grey egrets, red-tailed hawks and a variety of other birds visit from our kitchen window. Next, Brooks installed a greywater system around the house; water from the shower and the kitchen fed a pineapple guava tree in the backyard. Then, we put in more than fifteen fruit trees, and Brooks and Michael built a chicken coop, duck house and a chicken tractor out of recycled materials. I brought in laying hens, runner ducks and broilers for eggs and meat. I knew only a few things about poultry, but was willing to start small and teach myself further details. When I came across Patricia Foreman and Andy Lee's books on market gardening and poultry, I was eager to provide the best environment possible for our flock, so I contacted Patricia with chicken questions and was thrilled she quickly got back to me! Little did I know we shared many of the same interests and would one day become friends.

We put our poultry in what Permaculture would call Zone 2, close to the house where we could watch them from our kitchen window. It was a great spot; I got quite familiar with all their quirky habits. The runner ducks were some of the best entertainment we had on our homestead. A local nearby farm decided to replace raspberry bushes with peach trees, so Michael and I went out and dug up more than fifty raspberry bushes, and planted them alongside our poultry fence. Six months later we had delicious berries.

Before I took the PDC, concepts like, "What does the land want?" hadn't crossed my mind. It was an awareness that made me realize, "We are the Earth;" there's no separation. I couldn't help but wonder as a culture what we would do differently if all of us considered that deeper perspective when it came to land and the environment.

Thanks to Geoff and Darren in the design course, I learned how to make a Berkley Compost. I liked the fact that if I did it right, the compost was ready to be used in seventeen days. It was a specific blend of nitrogen, carbon, water, heat, and movement. Geoff said adding (timely) roadkill to our compost was a good nitrogen source, so if I discovered a dead owl on the road before the maggots did, I brought it home and added it to the compost. I passed up skunks and possums, but being a fan of owls, I rarely left them behind. Michael and I gathered loads and loads of alpaca manure, another nitrogen source, and used it continuously in our compost. I felt like a magician swirling our compost, adding ingredients, watering it, moving it, cooking it in the sun, and then planting with it. I picked up boxes of old food at our local health-food store for our ducks and chickens; whatever they didn't eat got added to our compost. Nothing was wasted.

Our cottage faced west and in summer, the sun penetrated the house, so in order to get it shaded, Brooks built a trellis and I planted grapes. Being a perennial, the house would still have access to the sun in winter and be shaded with food growing in summer. Every planting decision I made served more than one function, in permaculture it's called "stacking functions." It's a brilliant way of using resources, structures, and animals for more than one purpose.

I went down to the river and collected large rocks for an herb spiral, and a friend from Santa Barbara helped me build it. Herb spirals work great for people who don't have a lot of space to garden, and although that wasn't our situation, I was eager to build one simply for the experience. We put the spiral in what permaculture would call Zone 1 right outside our kitchen door. This way we didn't have to walk far early in the early morning to harvest herbs for our eggs! In addition to being aesthetically appealing, the pyramid-like design also creates a microclimate for a variety of different plants. The idea is to plant herbs that like full sunshine at the top of the spiral, and cooler-climate plants at the bottom part of the spiral.

We invited musicians, new friends, and locals over for potlucks and live music in our garden. It was fun providing a space for people to commune. There were a lot of special, talented people living in the valley. People were doing amazing things, like building their homes with their own hands.

Spirit Pine Sanctuary was just up the mountain from our homestead. Their beautiful structures are an awesome illustration of their gifts as artists. I got my hands dirty more than once helping people build small cob structures like ovens and greenhouses.

The timing of the PDC was perfect. I was introduced to more and more ways of living sustainably and I really felt my life move more in that direction. In addition, when I worked in the garden, I wasn't burdened by my health condition, but instead I was present, engaged and interested. My stamina improved and my connection to the earth with it. I felt empowered working the soil, sowing seeds, and cultivating food. I embraced my new lifestyle with all my heart.

A Cure and a Dance

Life in Santa Ynez was deeply fulfilling but despite my satisfaction with our sustainable lifestyle I was still frustrated with my health because symptoms of MCS kept increasing and I wanted to know why. If I was working out side in the garden and our neighbor did her laundry, the smells from her perfumed detergent made me weak and gave me an immediate headache. It was little things like this that I found unacceptable. I thought maybe a whole body detox was the next step to improving well being, so I rented an infrared sauna several days a week from Deb, a friend in the healing field.

Deb introduced me to Dr. Sherry Rogers' book, *Detoxify or Die*. Rogers credited her own recovery from MCS with a number of influences, including Dr. Rea at the Environmental Health Center in Dallas,Texas. It was the first time I'd heard of Dr. Rea and his center and I was ecstatic to discover his specialty is treating people with a variety of conditions related to toxic exposures. I thought for sure he held the key to my recovery from MCS. Since Michael's family lives in Texas, we combined a family visit with an appointment. I had high expectations for solutions regarding my health and I could hardly wait to meet Dr. Rea. I committed to spending five days at the Center. Every day, I tested to see what chemicals, food, mold, or pollen I was reacting to. The clinic was unique in that it offered preservative-free skin testing which is necessary for sensitive people. I was also given an immune-boosting shot to increase my white blood cell count, and a nutritionist designed an allergy-free rotational food plan with supplements which I followed when we returned home.

In our first meeting, Dr. Rea asked me a question no other person, doctor or practitioner had yet: "Where do you live?" I exclaimed with great satisfaction that our sweet homestead was located in beautiful wine country. Rea shook his head in disbelief and said, "You gotta move." I was taken back by his straightforward and brisk advice. He said my health would continue to decline as long as I lived around vineyards, orchards, and conventional farms that sprayed regularly with pesticides. He insisted the chemicals were a health hazard to everyone, but most importantly to someone like me with a toxic exposure (mold) in my past. Many times, I drove past conventional farms and vineyards when they were spraying. Workers wore white HazMat suits with large masks to protect themselves. It was a thought provoking sight and one I couldn't ignore; maybe he was right. But moving again wasn't something I wanted to think about. It seemed ludicrous to keep running from external conditions. There were a number of people living in the valley unaffected by the surroundings. In fact, many were healthy, vibrant, and strong. I wondered if there really was any "safe" place left in the world.

I appreciated Dr. Rea's insights, but at the end of my commitment I couldn't wait to leave the center. With the exception of a few kind people, I thought the staff at The Environmental Health Center lacked compassion and optimism. The best thing that came out of that experience was the awareness that, for some of us, living around agriculture is a health risk.

After we returned from the Environmental Health Center I needed something to take my mind off the fact that, not only was I unsuccessful finding a cure for MCS, but soon, we would move again. I decided if I couldn't live free of MCS, I was going to enjoy life regardless. Homesteading and permaculture were two hobbies that gave me a lot of personal satisfaction, but the next source of inspiration came through West African dancing and drumming. We were already fans of West African music and had been listening to musicians like Baaba Maal from Senegal, and Fela Kuti from Nigeria, for many years, but when we found Lisa Beck and Budhi Harlow and their performance group, Panzumo in Santa Barbara; we dove right into their courses. Michael took Budhi's drumming lessons and together we took Lisa's weekly dance class. I lacked the physical stamina at first for Lisa's West African Dance classes, but I stuck with it because it was exactly what I needed. For me, dancing is life giving. The rhythm, sweating, drums, the feeling of connection in my body; those classes had a sacred blend to them that affected me at my very core. When I danced, I tuned in to the resonance of well being. The pulse of the African drums penetrated my soul and made me feel alive. It took time and practice to get up to speed with the steps, but eventually I did. I looked forward to those classes every week, and tried to recruit friends in Santa Ynez to join us. The classes were an another source of creativity and inspiration in our lives.

Another Paradigm and New Territories

After we left King Hill Farm in Maine, our friends Jasmine and Eric stayed on as apprentices at Four Seasons, Elliot Coleman's farm. When their apprenticeship ended, they moved to Big Sur, California where they had a baby, started their own business, wrote a book on how to grow microgreens, and lost their home in a wildfire. They were on their way back East to start their dream farm when they stopped in to visit us on our homestead in Los Olivos.

A lot younger than Michael and me, Jasmine and Eric are two interesting young people with positive outlooks on life. Their son, Haven, reflected their bright spirits. He was full of life and unafraid to be himself. They are excellent parents and we were thrilled to learn they had a second baby on the way.

As always, when we got together with them we had some great conversations. They shared their understanding of the laws of the universe, namely, the law of attraction. In the past I had considered that sort of thinking as New Age propaganda. The idea that we "create our own reality" was a perspective that had never appealed to me. In fact, just the mention of that idea provoked the pessimist in me. Being an activist I was anti- this and anti-that. I pushed against people, places and things that I judged as wrong, and although my heart was in the right place, my dogmatic attitude created a split in my thinking, and left me in a state of constant resistance. The timing of their visit was auspicious. I was frustrated with my health and I wanted to feel better. It was time for new medicine.

Knowing them, they had no intention of converting Michael, me, or anyone else for that matter. In fact, the way they shared their personal perspectives on life was very subtle. What caught my attention was their consistently positive attitudes. They were manifesting opportunities that were bringing them closer and closer to their personal dreams. I was intrigued. If they could manifest their dreams why couldn't we? Their level of clarity and confidence in a promising future made me reconsider many personal beliefs. I decided I had nothing to lose by shifting my outlook on life. I devoured the positive medicine they left on our doorstep. Being curious, I read up on universal laws and day by day my attitude shifted. I was reintroduced to tools to help close the gap between being a physical being and a spiritual being, and from that point forward I understood the value of having some kind of daily mindful practice that connected me to the broader sense of living whole. After their visit I began to focus more on what made me feel good. I started to look for little things to appreciate, and I took time out everyday to meditate. But most importantly, I stopped listening to the news every day and as a result, I felt a resurgence for life almost immediately.

Being a seeker, I had been at a place of questioning the meaning of life many times before. In fact, I was only twelve years old when I stumbled upon Dr. Norman Vincent Peale's book, *The Power of Positive Thinking*, in the attic of our family home. I have no idea who it belonged to, probably Dad, but even then, I was eager to know the true meaning of life and the secret to being happy. Being young I lacked the life experience to know the depth of Peale's message, but I carried that book around with me for many years anyway.

My new lighthearted attitude brought me a tremendous amount of joy! Instead of being problem orientated, I became more solution orientated. It was a process of retraining my mind to pay attention to what I wanted from life, instead of what I didn't want. As simple as it sounds, it took some time and some discipline to erase old thought patterns and habits, but eventually I became less resistant. In fact, I started to understand the wisdom in allowing life to simply unfold. Michael was already three steps ahead of me on a path of least resistance. His instincts to go with the flow of things was always a helpful reminder for me.

Jasmine and Eric's example of the benefits of living life in a more optimistic way, along with my friend Katherine's advice to focus more on the positive things life offered, rekindled my spirit. Not only did my health and vitality improve, but I also felt more and more optimistic. Our friend's visit became a pivotal turning point in our lives. Eventually Michael and I entered another paradigm of thinking and living. We've never looked back!

Michael and I were curious to know where our next home would be, so we did some research and eventually visited several areas: Ashland, Oregon; Northern California; Bend, Oregon; and Sonora, California. Exploring various cities as possibilities for our new home was rewarding and educational, but we didn't feel compelled to run in the direction of any of them. We decided to stay put until the next step was irresistible.

When we manifested the opportunity to manage Polyface at Buxton Farm in rural Virginia in September 2010, I'm not sure who was more excited about our next adventure, us, or my Aunt Jo in Ohio. Right before we left The Santa Ynez Valley, she sent me an urgent note. Inside was an interpretation of the name Grace. Because she thought it matched what we were headed towards, she couldn't wait to share it with me. I was inspired by the meaning.

Grace: In Kabbalistic Synopsis. The letter Gimel means "camel" and represents travel in all its forms. In Grace this letter represents the most radical form of travel, that of exploration. One Hebraic equivalent of the name Grace is the word "paths," so it is possible Grace will have a role in the establishment of new routes in already-mapped territories for trade or vacation purposes. Of course, not everybody called Grace will be an explorer in the literal sense. However, all Graces will have an exploratory personality, daring, inventive, and always ready to take on the next challenge.

(Excerpt from *The Hidden Truth of Your Name, A Complete Guide To First Names and What They Say About The Real You*, by The Nomenology Project)

I was hopeful whoever took over our homestead in Los Olivos would continue to nurture the gardens, fruit trees and chickens. The cottage was on one acre, and had incredible potential, but as sweet as our homestead was, it was located a block from a highway and adjacent to an elementary school. The endless noise of cars, trucks and motorcycles day and night wore us down over time. The elementary school brought constant traffic and loud school buses. Many times I had to wait to work in the garden until the buses left because their diesel fumes were overbearing.

I notified my massage clients about the move, but saying goodbye to them wasn't easy. Massage is an intimate exchange, and I had built up a handful of wonderful clients, many of whom I would miss. Plus, I had no idea if or when massage would be part of my life again; I doubted seriously there would be time for it at Buxton Farm.

The day the moving van came up from Los Angeles, it was one hundred and fourteen degrees. Soaring temperatures left us soaking wet and by the time we finished packing the van it was only noon but we were exhausted. Those extreme temperatures weren't something we would miss. What we would miss was our friends and the dynamic energy of the left coast, but the joyful anticipation we felt for our next home dominated our thoughts. Leaving our one acre homestead for a thousand acre farm was terribly exciting! Together, we felt the promise of an exciting new beginning. We would be within driving distance of my parents and Aunt Jo, working the land alongside one of the most experienced sustainable farmers in our country, and stimulated by seasons again. In addition, we'd revel in the joy of meeting new faces and exploring different places, we'd learn to shepherd an entirely new territory of land, and we'd feel the satisfaction of raising food to feed not only ourselves, but others, too. What could possibly go wrong?

When we pulled away from our homestead, I was humbled. I knew there were things we would miss about the Santa Ynez Valley. Friends were a given, but there were other things we wouldn't know had special meaning until we were gone. That's just how life is. Sometimes the things we treasure the most, are the ones we take for granted.

We intended to spend time exploring the Grand Canyon as we made our way across the country, but that plan was interrupted because the campground on the South Rim was under construction. Generators hummed through the night, and loud machines blasted away during the day. The noise and congestion were unbearable. Our quest for quiet and solitude amplified our desire to get to Buxton Farm as soon as possible. We continued east to our place of refuge.

Part Four

"Double Rainbow in Spring, Buxton Farm 2011"

Buxton Farm 2010

We arrived at Buxton Farm in Bath County, Virginia, on October 3, 2010. It was a misty, rainy Sunday afternoon, and with the exceptions of Evan, a Polyface apprentice, we were the only two people on the farm. In no time at all Evan moved the herd, then headed back to Polyface Farm in Swoope.

From the time we committed to managing Buxton Farm, I wondered if my body would tolerate living in a 100-year-old farmhouse. Being sensitive to so many things, it was a concern I had when Joel gave us a quick tour of the house on our interview, and I carried that concern with me on our drive across the country to Virginia. But even if there were a few challenges, I trusted we would sort them out, because I felt solid in our decision to work with Joel and Daniel Salatin and Polyface Farms.

After we unpacked our car, I was anxious to get inside and see the condition of our new home. The house was in desperate need of fresh air, so I opened as many windows as I could, and I was disappointed to discover some of them were permanently jammed shut. How could anyone live in such a pristine setting and not take full advantage of all the fresh air?

Three hungry cats were left behind, and one of them jumped through the screen on our front door and ripped it wide open. As a result, flies and bugs flew freely into and throughout the entire house. After the previous farm manager and his family left, Polyface apprentices took turns living at Buxton. Fortunately they left behind a worn-out mattress. That funky pad along with our sleeping bags was our makeshift bed until the moving truck arrived with our personal items a week later. Our first week inside that old farmhouse felt like camping out.

My first priority was to clean the downstairs bathroom. Since it had a bathtub, I knew at the end of the day I would want to relax in a hot bath, so I removed a dirty old shower curtain and scrubbed the tub until it sparkled. Every time I ran hot water the smell of rotten eggs permeated the air. Not knowing yet that the water in that part of the county was high in sulfur, I thought there was something wrong with the well and immediately worried if the water was drinkable.

In the kitchen walls were painted a putrid bright green color which left the room cold and uninviting. Since Michael and I spend a lot of time cooking, we immediately decided that color would have to go. It was hard to decipher what color the linoleum floor in the kitchen originally was, perhaps white, but now it was dirty and permanently stained. Inside the refrigerator, I discovered frozen pig feet, generic bread, stale milk, a few half empty beer cans, and old cheese. The ghastly sight made me lose my appetite. I decided it was safer to leave our food in a cooler until we sterilized the inside of the refrigerator.

The hallway was partially painted a bright sky blue color which left me nauseous whenever I climbed the steps to the second floor. Upstairs in the three bedrooms, old funky windows had cracked panes with bugs and spiders living inside cavity windows. The stench of oil had permeated one bedroom, and gave me an instant headache, so we closed that room off for winter. We slept in each one of the bedrooms upstairs until we found the one most suitable for us, and as it turned out, the farm manager before us had remodeled it and used it as his master bedroom. It was the only insulated room in the house! In winter, that room withstood the force of incredible west winds, winds that kept us up all night. But our new bedroom also had wonderful views of the mountains, and in it we could hear the sweet sound of the creek meandering its way east into the pond behind the farmhouse. Outside our north window, we would eventually watch the herd and hens in the pasture alongside the creek. I always looked forward to them being in that pasture because their foraging sounds filled my heart with joy.

The entire house had hardwood floors that were beat up or painted over with dark colors. They had no appeal at all, but at least they weren't carpeted. Funky, stained carpet would have sent me over the edge.

In winter, we discovered that without any insulation downstairs, cold air came straight up through the cracks of the floors, and ventilated itself throughout the entire house like an outside breeze. Fortunately, we had two solid wood burning stoves to keep us warm; they were the best part of the farmhouse. The house was also set up for oil as an additional heat source, but it was an old, leaky system. There was no way my body would tolerate it, so we covered up all the vents with plastic.

Like the rest of Buxton Farm, that old farmhouse needed a lot of love. There wasn't anything romantic about; in my opinion it was bleak, uncomfortable and saturated with the feeling of abandonment. The manager before us arrived in January and left by July. I wondered if we too were doomed.

As I realized how much time and energy it would take to make the farmhouse feel like home, I wondered what we'd gotten ourselves into. Then, I thought of my sister Kerry in California, a woman who insisted on living neat and clean. If she were in my shoes, her desire for things to be spotless would have prevailed. Home or no home, she would have walked away.

My solar plexus rumbled, so I stepped outside on the front porch to soothe myself, and Michael joined me. The depth of neglect inside that farmhouse pierced both of us simultaneously. "We don't have to stay," Michael softly declared. Knowing exactly what to say in dire situations is one of the many reasons he's so easy to love. I knew where he was coming from, and he was right. But all I could think was, we came this far, we can't turn around.

We sat on the front porch and took in the beauty. I pondered acre after acre of open space. The endless mountain views were breathtaking. After a bit of reflection, I came to some conclusions. First, we didn't come for that old farmhouse; there was a bigger picture brewing inside of us. We came for the land, the animals, the silence, the peaceful setting, the adventure, and ultimately the personal expansion. And we didn't just haphazardly arrive at Buxton Farm. We were summoned. Being summoned to something is a different story. Everything inside of you says, "Hell yes"! As we sat on the front porch, I knew we had to focus on what Buxton was going to become for us, not what it was at that moment. We're used to breathing new life into old worn out places. It's what we do. We had to give that old farmhouse a wide berth. There was no room for doubt; we had to persevere.

The tender songs of rare birds along with the willow tree next to the creek eased our uncertainty. The sound of that creek was something we paid to hear in California. At Buxton Farm, water was everywhere. Just outside that old farmhouse was a garden of Eden, a nature lover's paradise. We reveled in the luxury of not seeing or hearing one neighbor. As the horrific details we'd discovered inside the house were overshadowed by the setting, I knew we were right where we were supposed to be; life wasn't testing us. We were taking on this opportunity because we knew it would be adventurous. The truth is, following your bliss takes courage. There are no guarantees. After we regrouped, we went back inside and got busy in our new home.

The moving company arrived with our things about a week after we did. The driver said the semi was too big for our driveway, so we unloaded our belongings into our small farm truck a mile from the farmhouse. Fortunately, Joel and a former apprentice were at Buxton that same day cutting firewood for us. Winter was right around the corner. Thanks to them, large items like our non toxic natural rubber latex mattress got carried upstairs into our bedroom without anyone getting injured. Their visit was good timing. Joel lifted and maneuvered heavy items into the house without flinching.

The truck driver lived in Los Angeles, California and was blown away by Buxton's beauty. He confessed he slept soundly the night before in the moving truck on the side of the road. It had been years since he'd seen so many stars at night. He was envious of our new home. I knew where he was coming from. After living in Los Angeles for fourteen years, Buxton Farm did indeed resemble paradise.

We warmed the house by painting the sitting room, kitchen, dining room, living room, hallway, and our bedroom with mostly soft colors. The house hardly received any sun in winter, which was dreadful, so we kept a few walls white to attract more light. We cleaned out the mudroom, and painted it, too. We scrubbed the kitchen floor, cleaned the oven and all the cabinets. I went through gallon after gallon of white vinegar scrubbing walls and mopping floors. We slept with windows open to refresh the stale air, even if it was twenty degrees outside. We hung a few of our paintings and put curtains up in an effort to make some of the rooms feel more like home. Kip and her brothers, Dick and Dave, the farm owners, made a few improvements on the house, which we really appreciated. They put new screen doors on the front and back doors and installed two new windows in the master bedroom upstairs. Those windows helped in winter when the cold air and west winds were constant. Month after month, the inside of the house came together. That old farmhouse contained stories. A lot of different people lived within those walls; a history of different families. As we settled into our new home, I could feel our presence adding to the memories.

I was on a mission to move energy inside and outside; open things up. Outside in the yard, I tore down an old fence where previous renters put their dogs. All the fences and gates around the house felt stifling so whatever I could remove I did. I found used patio furniture for free on Craigslist, which came in handy for summer meals outside with apprentices.

The three cats left behind adopted us. Not being cat people, we were surprised how quickly they grew on us. When Michael named each of them, I knew they had become part of the family. Tennessee, who we called Tenny, was named after Tennessee Williams. Budhi, the youngest and toughest, was named after Michael's West African drum teacher in Santa Barbara, and Augustus, who we called Gussy, was named after one of our favorite actors, Robert Duvall, and his character from the miniseries "Lonesome Dove". The cats were slightly feral, yet at times a little needy. They were also fierce hunters, and although I preferred they catch mice only, I learned over time that they killed birds, rabbits, squirrels and even some of our baby chicks. I drew the line our second season after we caught Budhi inside our poultry brooder eating our day-old chicks.

One night in the early days at Buxton, a wild animal made a fierce cry. The sound penetrated the dark black night. Inside the farmhouse, I was terrified. It was hard to pinpoint exactly what it was. With the National Forest adjacent to us, the list of possible suspects could go on and on. The following day we told the apprentices at Polyface about it, and they all snickered to themselves. Not one of them was surprised. Some of them lived at Buxton at one point during the high season before we arrived, and they never forgot it! There was something about Buxton's remote and untamed location. I'm certain each of them slept with a gun within reach. I was amazed at one female intern who was brave enough to sleep at Buxton Farm alone. When I asked her how she did it, she said she moved the mattress into the kitchen, and slept with a gun next to her with all the lights on, then called her mom in California and talked until she fell asleep. I totally understood her fear, and I told Michael there was no way I could stay at Buxton by myself.

The apprentices recommended we purchase a firearm for Buxton, but it was too soon for us to consider. I had opinions about guns; investing in one would be another wait-and-see decision for us, like almost everything our first year. Luckily, Daniel Salatin let us borrow one of his and it came in handy throughout the year with predators.

We had space for countless animals, which was tempting for me, but we decided our first year would be a wait-and-see year, so reluctantly, I suspended my desire to get any pets. Without knowing how things would pan out, I had to be patient. I made an agreement with Michael the only animals our first year would be the ones we agreed to raise for Polyface.

Michael picked up where Joel and his former apprentice left off cutting firewood. Chain saws intimidate me, so after Michael cut the wood I followed behind him in our truck and collected it. Harvesting firewood became an outdoor activity I enjoyed not only because of the physical exercise, but also because it gave us the opportunity to familiarize ourselves with the land.

There was a very large garden next to the house, but it was totally overgrown with brush and weeds when we arrived. For years, no one had tended it, so I hired a neighbor and he came over on his tractor and bush hogged the entire garden. It felt great to have years of old brush cleared away. It was thrilling to have another kitchen garden and I was eager to discover what could grow in Bath County, Virginia.

October is a good time of the year to build soil for the following spring, and since we had plenty of cardboard boxes left over from our move, we used them for sheet mulching the garden. Michael and I broke them down and soaked them in water, then placed them on top of the soil in the garden, then we brought tractor loads of chicken fertilizer, a nitrogen source from the poultry brooder, and put it on top of the cardboard. After that we planted winter rye as a cover crop, and waited in anticipation for spring when we would see lots of new worms in the soil underneath the cardboard.

Getting Acquainted

Living in Virginia never crossed our minds before Buxton Farm. In fact, moving there was an option only because we wanted to work with Polyface Farms; the open space and beauty was an added bonus. The mountain views were stunning, but especially in fall. Michael and I loved how freeway traffic flowed without congestion. Sometimes we would be the only car on the interstate for miles. In many other states, freeways turned into parking lots, but that was never an issue for us in Virginia.

In addition to the fantastic scenery, we also appreciated how people in the South seemed to move at a slower, friendlier pace. The intensity of the West was replaced with people who looked us in the eye in check-out lines, for example. The small towns in our area had a sort of "mom-and-pop" feeling. It took some getting used to being called "ma'am." It made me feel older than my years. Michael tried to reassure me it was simply a Southern expression of respect, but I never got used to it.

In California, if we weren't growing what we ate, we purchased most of our food at local farmers' markets, which were open every season, but in Virginia it was a different story. Large corporate grocery store chains were sometimes the best we could do. I don't know exactly why but for some reason I feel invisible inside those oversized stores. It took time for me to get comfortable shopping in them. The closest suitable one to us was in Staunton, Virginia, which was a little over an hour from Buxton. It was a long haul back to civilization if we forgot something, so we became very efficient list makers.

Buxton Farm is in Millboro, Virginia and is part of Bath County, a very small county with less than 5,000 residents. In winter, we often went to Warm Springs Library for good books and a short reprieve from the farm. The staff was friendly and quick to offer their advice on directions and different things to do and explore in the area. One of the older librarians was from the South and had lived in Bath County for several years. Her first advice to us was not to gossip about anyone we befriended in our neighborhood because everyone somewhere down the line was related. We were reminded of her sound advice a week later when we were running errands in Staunton, and we met a family from our neck of the woods. When they asked how things were going at Buxton, I mentioned we were waiting patiently for the local plumber to return our phone call, but since it had been several days, I was slightly distressed it was taking him so long to respond. They just smiled and informed me the plumber was their father. Michael shook his head and looked the other way. After that incident, I followed the librarian's golden rule.

Hot Springs, Virginia, the only city in Virginia without a traffic light, was just over the mountain from us. It is a very charming town, with the Homestead Resort as its centerpiece. The Homestead is a five star resort with a variety of amenities. Over twenty American presidents have stayed at the historic resort, and for some, it was a golfers' paradise. It's the biggest employer in the area, and keeps Bath County on the map. We discovered they had "high tea" every afternoon, and whenever we had free time we stopped in to enjoy it. In addition to the Homestead, we discovered live music at Garth Newel Music Center. Like almost every place in Bath County the music center was beautiful and inviting. In summer, they hosted a music festival on the lawn of their property, and in winter we were entertained by a number of fabulous visiting and resident musicians.

Arriving in October was perfect, not only because of the spectacular beauty of fall colors, but also because it gave us a few months to get acquainted with the herd before they returned to Polyface for winter. It was impossible for them to spend the winter at Buxton because all of the water lines were above ground. That was good news for us because dealing with frozen water lines during ice and snowstorms was one thing we didn't want on our plate.

I took an immediate liking to Tonya, the leader cow. She was a Brahman cow, older than the rest of the herd, and she was beautiful. Polyface kept her around because she knew how to lead the herd efficiently. Her enormous body swayed from side to side when she moved. It was a walk that conveyed she knew who she was. Tonya was all business. Every day between four and six, she waited patiently for us to arrive. She watched every move Michael made until we opened the gate to the her next salad bar. If we ran late, she let us know she wasn't happy. Her bellow sent shivers up our spines. We learned to depend on her when we moved cattle across the river, down the road a few miles, and through the swamp. Her golden color and magnificent set of horns set her apart from the rest of the herd. Tonya became our gal!

Joel and Daniel forewarned us about Carl, Buxton's caretaker. They claimed he was a long-winded storyteller who could talk for hours. When we first met him his Appalachian accent was deep and thick, he was almost impossible to understand. A few times he had to repeat himself. I learned to watch his lips as he spoke, and eventually I made sense of almost everything he said.

Carl was good friends with the previous farm manager at Buxton and when that family left, he was disappointed. When he heard we were coming from California, he wasn't sure what to expect, so he took his time getting to know us. We went through a period of initiation with not only him, but his buddies who hunted and fished at Buxton all their lives. There was a short window of time when Michael and I definitely felt like the new kids on the block.

Carl was also our go-to person regarding Buxton, and the only person who knew Buxton Farm intimately. He grew up down the street and had worked on the farm since he was a kid. At one time he lived in the farmhouse with his wife Norma and their children, and farmed the land full time with cows and crops. Carl and Norma were a big part of Buxton's history, and in time, they both became very dear to us.

In early spring our local radio station advertised community road kill potlucks. Unfortunately we were too busy to get to one. Carl assured us that groundhogs, squirrels and raccoons were quite tasty. I was sorry I couldn't find out for myself. Attending one of those gatherings would have been another interesting experience to add to our list of rural adventures.

Our Tiny

A couple of years before we moved to Virginia, we visited a woman in Bend, Oregon, who was building her version of a "Tiny Tumbleweed House," small portable structures built on flatbed trailers. I found Leslie through a network of people living with MCS. Like me, she suffered from sick building syndrome, so there were few places she could visit without her body reacting. Since the mold exposure, I had struggled with the same issue, and like Leslie, I was eager to take matters into my own hands and build a place where I could comfortably live full-time.

Leslie considered her nontoxic tiny studio her "safe" space. Michael and I drove to Bend, Oregon, and stayed in it. Her portable space had high ceilings, a loft, a small office, and a swing on the front porch. It was tiny and very cozy. She had a talent for good design, and her research on nontoxic materials was extensive. We appreciated Leslie for sharing her ideas with us. Impressed with her work and longing for a similar space of our own, we couldn't wait to get back to California and find someone to build one for us. But when we returned, we couldn't find anyone in our area who understood the alternative materials that were needed for the space to be truly nontoxic. We decided the timing wasn't right, and let it rest.

In Virginia, we discovered a fantastic skilled woodworker, an expert in his craft. It turned out he also knew about tiny homes and was very interested in building one. We'd found our guy! The synchronicity of finding him was another serendipitous experience our first season at Buxton. The best part about our small space (120 square feet) was that it would be built on a trailer so that when we left Buxton, it could go with us. It was very exciting for us to think about owning something of our own.

By December, we had purchased a brand new flatbed trailer, measuring eight feet wide by sixteen feet long. I spent the winter researching ideas, designs, nontoxic materials, window choices, color palettes and insulation options. Like Leslie, we decided to make our tiny studio, without interior walls. This way it could become a bedroom, a guest room, office, meditation nook, or massage studio.

Our portable space took some time to come together, but the builder's precision and love of his work were key ingredients. Together we decided on high ceilings, large windows, stained glass, ceiling fan, and a small loft. Since the tiny was our first time designing a building, we trusted his opinions and experience, but we didn't always agree on what was green and what was truly nontoxic. Anyone living with MCS will tell you there's a big difference between the two. It took patience and a great deal of communication from both sides. The research was educational and at times, grueling.

Designing and building the tiny was another entirely new experience that we added to our plate during our first year in Virginia. It was an incredibly busy time. Since it was being built on the builder's property where his workshop was located, whenever we could get away from the farm we drove over and worked on it with him. Often it was short blocks of time in between farm chores.

I was so glad I took the time to observe patterns of the sun our first winter because we knew where to put our tiny studio so that it was in a south facing part of the farm, and would get sun all day. Daniel Salatin chose the exact spot for the tiny so that it was out of the way of the herd, trucks, and tractors.

At the end of August, the tiny came home to Buxton and I couldn't wait to spend time in it. In spite of using as many nontoxic products as possible, surprisingly my body reacted to the (new) poplar and maple wood terpene smells. I was disappointed I was unable to move into it right away. Throughout the day and on nights without rain, we kept all the windows open, and in time most of those smells dissipated. Then we hired an electrician to connect the tiny to the power source in the barn so that we had heat and electricity. The following spring we moved our bed inside and slept there the rest of the season.

Our tiny sat on a small hill overlooking the broiler and turkey field where Jack, our guard dog fended off packs of coyotes almost every night. Sleeping so closely to wildlife and the farm animals was perfect for us. The sound of the river was just outside our front door, along with a pair of eagles that soared along the riverbed almost every day. We had great views of the property and we spotted deer, rabbits, skunks, groundhogs, coyotes, raccoons, and fox from our windows. Sleeping in our tiny in its secluded spot was a magnificent feeling, second to owning something of our very own.

Shooting Stars

I spent a great deal of our first winter in Virginia walking the forest, even though it was an icy cold winter, I walked several hours every day. Without those walks, I would have been unable to live inside the moldy farmhouse. For some unknown reason the wood burning stove activated symptoms of MCS. My solution for migraines or brain fog was long walks in the woods. The fresh air cleared my head and my mind. Sometimes Michael joined me. I'm certain we made our way across Buxton's one thousand acres, and then some. We explored every bit of that farm. It was an extraordinary feeling to live on so much land, and a privilege to live with a national forest all around us. With so much anticipation of the first season, I familiarized myself with that land long before we put hundreds of animals on it. But, looking back, I wish I had paced myself. I hiked in big muck boots that had absolutely no support for my feet. Day after day, treading over pastures, snow, and ice destroyed my right foot. I don't know how I did it, but I spent the next two years working the land with a chronically injured and painful foot.

Quite frequently in spite of freezing temperatures we took walks after dinner. The crisp fresh evening air in winter was deeply invigorating. Many times the farm was blanketed in snow but inclement weather didn't stop us. Seeing the stars and all phases of the moon was irresistible. In fact, since no one else lived on the farm we took advantage of the spectacular views of the land from the main house. On clear nights we bundled up, took a seat on the hillside and waited until one of us saw a shooting star. Rarely were we disappointed!

Gloomy winter days from time to time were fine for us. But if we got into a spell of long periods with no hint of sunshine at all, I got a little cranky. After living on the West Coast for nearly twenty years, it's impossible for me to thrive without Sunshine Vitamin D. With a fair amount of time on our hands in winter, we took advantage of the down time and read.

The first book I read was *Still Grazing, The Musical Journey of Hugh Masekela*, a South African musician. I was drawn to his autobiography, and had become enthralled with his music and lyrics after I had the privilege of seeing his outstanding band perform in Campbell Hall at UCSB with my good friend, and dancing partner Dana Di Croce-Hartley.

"Stimela" is one of his more popular songs. This song tells the story of the coal trains in South Africa that carried weary workers to the mines to dig for diamonds. Workers were taken away from their families, lived in filthy conditions, and were paid a scanty sum to toil all day for something they would never own. When Masekela played that ballad in Santa Barbara, the entire audience was transfixed.

In his autobiography, Masekela recounted how apartheid had affected his life, his family and friends. I loved reading his story and learning more about the people of South Africa who fought for their freedom. Naturally he wrote a song about Madiba, Nelson Mandela; one of my favorite champions. Masekela's book was one of many that distracted me from dreary days and bitter cold temperatures. To this day, I enjoy his music.

In the heart of winter, Canadian geese gathered on the pond behind the farmhouse. They had a specific routine: awaken at dawn, set out to forage, and return early evening, just before sundown. The farm was very quiet in winter, so I welcomed the activity of their comings and goings. Most of them had companions, but every once in awhile we'd see an unusual solo goose. The pond they inhabited brought in all sorts of interesting wildlife. Every season was different: beautiful grey herons, wild turkeys and ducks, snapping turtles, frogs, carp, perch, white egrets and more.

When winter was over, local hunters were looking forward to fishing in Buxton's pond, but they claimed the fish in the pond were outnumbered by snapping turtles, so they decided to eliminate as many turtles as possible. Men with guns gathered on the edge of the pond, shot the turtles, then left them to die in the grass. It was an activity that bothered me because it seemed so unnecessary. These men had been hunting and fishing at Buxton almost all their lives, being the new kid on the block I wasn't in a position to interfere. Somehow I gathered enough courage to request they keep the number of turtle shootings to a minimum, and much to my surprise they took my request to heart.

In January 2011, Daniel and a few Polyface apprentices came to Buxton to set up a new hoop house for our laying hens. Temperatures were in the upper teens with an intense wind chill factor that day, but we worked anyway. The hoop house was large and required strong hands and able bodies to assemble. Once we got it put together, we hired a lumber company to deliver several truckloads of wood chips, and then Polyface brought over 600 laying hens. I was delighted to be surrounded by poultry once again. Within our flock of 600 hens we discovered eight roosters. We waited for a warm day, butchered six of the roosters, and slow cooked them throughout the season. They were tender and delicious.

I have a weakness for laying hens. Their distinct personalities quickly win me over. You might think 600 of them would be too much for two people, but not for me. More than once, I lost track of time sitting inside the hoop house watching them scurry around. They were great entertainment. Their songs filled the farm with new energy, and every morning I looked forward to tending them. Each one of our girls held a special place in my heart.

One hen, however, had me concerned. Whenever I walked into the hoop house, she ran towards me and jumped up as if she wanted me to carry her, like a pet, in my arms. In addition, she didn't seem to care too much for her five hundred and ninety sisters. Over time they detected her attitude towards them and started picking on her. I knew if I didn't do anything, the pecking order of the flock would overpower her, and she would become a victim. I didn't have many options until Kip, the farm owner, introduced me to her friend, Patricia Foreman, Lexington, Virginia's "Chicken Whisperer." I had come across Pat's books when we lived in California, but I had no idea she lived in Virginia and was a friend of Kip's. It was another serendipitous experience at Buxton Farm. One winter Sunday afternoon, I attended one of Pat's chicken homesteading classes and was introduced to her beloved traveling partner, Oprah Hen-Free. Pat and Oprah Hen-Free traveled around together educating people about raising chickens. When I told Pat about our pet chicken, she offered to adopt her. I was so relieved. With fewer girls to hassle her on Pat's homestead, she stood her ground and immediately became part of the flock. Pat named her Gracie.

Tonya, leader cow.

Getting Started and Crossing the River

For our first season at Buxton Farm we contracted with Polyface to raise and manage four thousand broilers, three hundred turkeys, six hundred laying hens, and three hundred head of cattle. They owned all the animals and provided the feed for the poultry. In exchange for moving their cows and the eggmobile daily, they paid our rent and utilities. For profit we sold eggs and broilers directly back to them.

The herd of 300 cattle arrived, and by mid-March we received our first batch of 500 broilers. Ridgeway Hatchery drove thousands of chicks from Ohio to Polyface for them, us, and other satellite farms. Picking our chicks up at Polyface was a wonderful way to receive large numbers of chicks without having to wait for their arrival in the mail or hunt them down at the post office. Every three weeks until August, a batch of 500 chicks waited for us on Thursday afternoons at Polyface Farm.

We brought our first batch home to Buxton in late March and put them in the brooder for three weeks, until April; when they were old enough to go out in broiler pens in pasture. Flooding was rampant that first spring and more than once, we rescued our chicks from high water and damp conditions. The risk of doing nothing was too high, because those meat birds were a significant part of our paycheck.

Working with the herd day after day, even if it was only thirty minutes, was an effortless way of building trust and establishing a relationship with them. Daniel taught us a simple "cowie" call that the herd responded to when it was time for them to move to new pasture. When Carl, our neighbor, watched us move the herd, he teased us and said they acted more like dogs because everyday we "fooled with them."

Joel and Daniel had been farming all their lives; getting up to speed with their standards took planning. Walking pastures to observe grass with them was fast paced and my favorite part of their visits. I enjoyed listening to them talk about the quality of specific grasses in the fields, and I was constantly impressed with Daniel Salatin's knowledge. Much younger than us in years, his expertise about cows and his fearless attitude were impressive. We could see why Joel and Teresa were so proud of him. Daniel knew something about everything.

A lot of our time was spent observing the animals, land, climate and weather patterns. It took time for us to feel like honest shepherds but if we paid close attention the animals always let us know their needs. Eventually, we established a rhythm with them. One of the best surprises about managing Buxton Farm was how knowledgeable we became about intensive grazing. Polyface was in their third year of leasing Buxton Farm when we arrived, and the positive impact of the herd in those early years was starting to pay off. It was obvious the mineral content of the soil had increased since they initially began leasing the land. Michael figured out the intensive-grazing system with great care and observation. In time, we watched cows turn pastures into luscious fertile ground. Witnessing the positive effect of proper management of land and grass with the herd was something we wanted to share with everyone.

Michael and I got a bit anxious one week in spring when the cows were across the river and the rain would not cease. In April, Bath County had flood warnings every other day. It was a sharp contrast to go from dry California to nonstop downpours our first spring. The herd needed to be moved back to pasture on our side of the river, but with the water level getting higher and higher, we started to wonder exactly how to pull it off.

The day finally came when the herd had no salad bar left, and so Tonya, the leader cow, gathered the herd and waited across the river for us at the gate. It was our first time moving the herd across the river, so Daniel came out to assist us. He's a true cowboy, but when he saw how high & swiftly moving the river was, he got nervous. The only way to get to the herd was the swinging bridge, and Daniel Salatin hated that bridge because it was old, unsteady and very unstable. As he inched his way across, Michael gathered up the herd, and I called them from across the river, motioning them to move where the water level was lowest. It took a tremendous amount of focus and prompting to get 300 head of cattle to follow my lead. When Tonya, the leader cow, eased her way into the fast-moving river, the current immediately took her a little downstream, but she knew exactly how to steady herself. She followed my antics and made it safely across. With our lead gal across, we were in good shape. I'm sure the rest of the herd decided if that old broad can do this, then we can, too. Fortunately they followed. Once the herd was across the river, they immediately shook off the drama and began eating their next salad bar as if nothing really significant had happened. Clearly, it was harder on us than it was on them.

This wouldn't be the last time the river was overflowing with the herd on the other side. Later in the season, it happened again and this time Joel came out to assist us. In anticipation of safely getting the herd across the river, when Joel arrived, I asked him if he was ready for the move. He quickly responded, "If I'm not, I better change my attitude." That's what I love about Joel, his can-do attitude makes everything seem possible.

High Season Schedule and House Guests

During the high season, daylight arrives early in Virginia, as a result; our workday started at 5:30 a.m. The first early morning chore was to move the hens' house (eggmobile) with the tractor, let them out, and replenish their food and water. Since they followed the cows, some mornings we moved them two miles down the country road. The hens had an wonderful life, free-ranging in green fertile pastures, catching bugs, eating grass, finding worms, and devouring fly maggots in the herds manure. From time to time, if we didn't put Jack, the guard dog, with the flock, we lost a few to aerial predators or a lone coyote hunting during the day, but for the most part, their lives were unbeatable, and their dark orange colored egg yolks were evidence.

After the hens, we checked the herd. First, we made sure none of them were out. Some of those rascals were good at jumping fence lines. Other times during the night, deer would knock down our portable fences and the herd would move into new pasture before it was time. Every morning, we made sure their water tanks were full with water flowing from our main source. The cows traveled across 300 acres of pasture, so water had to travel far to reach them. More than once, we spent an entire Sunday chasing water leaks through the forest. Michael walked the line through the forest, and I followed behind as closely as I could in the truck, listening for him to tell me when he found the leak. Sometimes it took hours until he found it. That wasn't how we wanted to spend Sundays, so we became vigilant and checked the water lines daily. Eventually, Michael mastered the system.

Next, we headed to the broiler field where we moved, fed, and watered chickens in seventeen broiler pens. Our arms got super strong from lifting and carrying five-gallon buckets of water and feed. I always looked for ways to use the leverage of my body. One of Joel's basic rules is to carry two five-gallon water buckets instead of one. By balancing out the weight of things we decreased the risk of straining our backs. Little things like this made a huge difference in maintaining our strength and agility.

Jack, a Livestock Guardian Dog (Akbash / Anatolian Shepherd), protected our poultry, but he came with a few bad habits we tried to eliminate. Every once in awhile, he would get through a fence and head down the driveway to the main road, which was really dangerous. We would get a call that he'd been found in the middle of the road, then someone would pull up to the farm with him in their backseat. Jack loved the attention and often hesitated before getting out of strangers' cars. It was a miracle he never got hit by a car or truck on the main road. He was a working dog but he loved being around people. In fact, he worked better and bonded more with us when we gave him attention. Jack worked nights and often slept during the day. Buxton couldn't exist without him. I became terribly fond of him.

We kept our turkeys in electrified mobile feathernets and moved them every other day. Because they were super curious about everything, often they got out and it was a bit of a dance to herd them back in. Watching them move to fresh pasture was entertaining because they were incredible grasshopper foragers. In summer, the farm was loaded with all sorts of bugs they enjoyed. The turkeys also had a strange tendency to be really cruel to one another. The pecking order was well intact. If one was wounded, others would gang up on the injured turkey and beat it up until it died. The first time we witnessed their bullying, we were stunned. In a way, they exhibited a gang-like mentality. It was hard for me to stand back and do nothing, so we pulled wounded turkeys aside and put them in broiler pens until they were strong enough to fend for themselves.

Inside the brooder, we housed the baby chicks and turkey poults. A normal batch was 500 chicks with 100 turkeys. The brooder was large and layered with sawdust. The chicks and turkey poults had plenty of room to roam around and explore. We had overhead propane heaters that worked well, but monitoring the temperature inside the brooder was important, especially for the turkeys because they were more fragile than the broilers. We learned they preferred a warmer environment. We had nipple waterers, which the poultry got accustomed to shortly after their arrival. Because the herd of cows was much more interesting, apprentices weren't inspired to learn about the brooder, so I became the poultry brooder monitor. I enjoyed watching how quickly the chicks and turkey poults grew.

We'd planted about thirty tomato plants in the hoop house in March, as soon as our laying hens left for pasture, so our final morning chore was harvesting our tomatoes, basil, and okra from the hoop house. The tomatoes loved the nitrogen fertilizer the hens left behind from winter, and we enjoyed growing tomatoes inside because blight was never an issue. When the tomatoes were mature, we intentionally stressed them by watering them less, only once every fourteen days. As a result, they were large, sweet, and delicious. I started canning as early as late June, and whatever tomatoes were left over we sold on Saturdays at the Hot Springs Farmers Market. It was crucial for us to work in the hoop house early because by 10:00 a.m. it turned into a sauna.

Without any glitches, like water leaks, morning chores took us about two hours. We usually returned to the house for breakfast, sometime between 8:00-9:00 a.m. Our early morning workout was much healthier than going to the gym. On the land we had fresh air, songbirds, sunshine, rain, and the sound of the glorious river. In summer, early morning fog lingered from the river, making a great buffer for the afternoon heat. If it was super hot, sometimes I took a dip in the river before breakfast. It was a great way to start the day. Having the river to swim in was a luxury other Polyface satellite farms didn't share, and we didn't take it for granted. We encouraged apprentices to take advantage of it as much as possible. It was the quickest route to refreshing our energy and attitudes.

We always planned to work before or after the hottest part of the day, so after breakfast if we weren't scheduled to process our chickens, Michael tended the herd, and I worked in the garden harvesting, weeding, and sowing. Polyface provided us with portable fencing so that we could move the herd every day. The stakes and rolls of wire went with us everywhere on that farm. Michael would walk the next pasture the herd was moving into and evaluate the grass. Then he'd decide how large to make their grazing area, and set up the next pasture with the portable fencing. If we were moving the herd across the river or down the road a few miles, then we set up bluff lines, a blue vinyl line that the cows could see. Bluff lines were used to prevent cows from straying to other pastures or into the forest. The herd got accustomed to staying within the lines, so it was a great tool.

Moving the herd two miles down the road was an all-day event. Sometime trees fell on fence lines, so that required chainsaw work. Other times there would be water issues. Eventually we learned not to move the herd until we were certain their water source was flowing. With every move, we provided minerals for the herd, but if the quality of grass was good, the cows didn't look twice at their supplements. They got what they needed from the pasture.

If there was a sick cow it would be separated from the rest of the herd and put in the barn with a buddy for a few days of rest. Sometimes we divided smaller cows into a separate heard and moved them closer to the farmhouse so that they could graze at their own pace. It was less stressful on them and having them closer to us made it easier to keep an eye on them. After about two weeks, we would reintegrate them into the larger herd.

More than once we went out to check the herd and found a baby calf. In every case like this, those particular moms were too young to be mothers and would abandon their babies. As much as I would have loved to nurse a calf, there just wasn't time. Waking in the middle of the night to bottle feed was something I couldn't commit to during the season. Fortunately, Norma and Carl were farmers who had lots of experience raising calves, so they were thrilled to adopt newborns.

Every two weeks, we had on average, 450 broilers to butcher, and since Buxton was the only Polyface satellite farm with its own processing area, we had the privilege of staying home and butchering. Without enough freezer space for all birds, we had to split the batches into thirds and process them on three different days of the week. Eventually we learned three people could process one hundred birds in two hours, but we preferred to work with at least five people.

Our normal chicken processing routine was that Michael or apprentices butchered the birds and I gutted them. It was a job I didn't mind, except when Daniel and Joel showed up on processing day; then I felt compelled to gut faster! Joel held the record for gutting a bird, and Daniel's wife Sheri was either right behind him or even faster; gutting chickens in their presence was always a little unnerving for me because I wanted to keep up with them! I was careful not to gut too fast because we used razor blades as knives, and they were very sharp. Unfortunately, several of us slashed our fingertips more than once.

On our homestead in California, we recited a short blessing before we butchered poultry; *"By the same power that slays you, I too am slain and and I too shall be consumed. For the law that delivers you into my hand shall deliver me into a mightier hand. Your blood and my blood is naught but the sap that feeds the tree of heaven."* It was part of a poem from Kahlil Gibran's book, *The Prophet: On Eating and Drinking.* I got the idea to say that short poem when I read Barbara Kingsolver's book, *Animal, Vegetable Miracle, A Year of Food Life.* Sometimes I said the blessing out loud at Buxton before we processed, and other times I said it to myself. Either way I always said it because it was important for me to come from a place of appreciation and reverence for animals before taking their lives.

After butchering the birds, we soaked them in cold water, then iced them. Michael composted all the chicken offal while we cleaned the processing area. It was always a good feeling to wrap up processing day. It wasn't a job for everyone, but for me it was tolerable because I enjoyed the momentum we got into with co-workers, and I appreciated being outside surrounded by so much beauty while we worked.

Every few months, we had deliveries of wood chips, which we mixed into the compost as our carbon source. Between the heat and the rain, the offal broke down within days, but we did have to electrify the compost pile to keep predators like raccoons and possums out. After lunch, we bagged the birds and froze them. Eventually we delivered the chickens to Polyface along with our eggs for them to market.

In our kitchen garden, I had summer squash, lettuce, carrots, beets, cilantro, peas, brassicas, chard, beans, spinach, strawberries, and asparagus. I sowed new seeds every ten days. Like the farmhouse, the garden was in a wind tunnel, so on windy days plants took a beating. The kitchen garden was really large and had great potential, but I kept it small and manageable, and as a result we enjoyed a sufficient harvest of different vegetables.

Our bodies changed dramatically during the high season. Between the demands of being on our feet all day, and working in the humidity, we were often drenched with sweat, so Michael and I both lost a significant amount of weight our first season. We were also hard our bodies and our farm clothes, pants got ripped on fence lines, shoes were worn out from manure and rain, and shirts easily torn and stained. Michael went through Carhartt pants in no time at all.

I enjoyed being able to do as much as the guys on the farm, so I learned how to drive a tractor, butcher chickens, set up fence lines, drive an ATV, use a Leatherman, carry a fifty-pound battery across pastures, and much to my surprise I even learned how to shoot a gun. I'm sure I could have even wrestled a cow to the ground if push came to shove. Keeping up with the rest of the crew helped me become stronger in every way.

We were the only couple to come on board with Polyface without apprenticing with them first. It's hard to define exactly where we cultivated the courage and stamina to take on Buxton Farm. It challenged us in so many unfamiliar ways. On our homestead in California, Michael and I worked in our garden together building soil, butchering our poultry, planting trees, sowing seeds, and then we went our separate ways to individual jobs and activities. But at Buxton, we had very few breaks from one another and little time to ourselves. Between the demands of the animals and living and working with people, our relationship was challenged more than once. Even though we deeply love one another, being together all the time took some patience and creativity, mostly because we see things and do things very differently. We constantly had to negotiate the best way to get things accomplished.

Furthermore, we weren't the first couple to feel challenged at Buxton Farm. Two other families had lived on the farm before us. The first couple got divorced during their first year, and the second family lasted six months. In the middle of our first season I began to understand why they were not able to manage the stress of running Buxton Farm. The work was physically demanding, and the land was vast. Cows could be two miles down the road, hens up on the hill, and the broilers and turkeys out by the river. Managing three hundred acres in pasture with poultry and cows took specific planning and strategy. You had to know how to pace yourself, and in a deeper sense, had to feel, as if the land, animals, and you were connected.

In addition to the demands of managing hundreds of acres of land, the farm was extremely remote. Every family that tried to manage Buxton Farm struggled with feeling isolated. Social networking in that part of the country is centered around church; we were living in the Bible Belt, and no matter how much we wanted to feel community, going to church wasn't one of our strategies for meeting people

Even though I loved the experience we were having, it wasn't long before I missed our community of friends on the West Coast. When Shelley, our good friend from Santa Ynez made the long trek out to Buxton from California our first season, I was thrilled. Her timing was perfect. Things were super intense on the farm. I had made some naive decisions about working and living with people and as a result; I was struggling with the lack of privacy in our personal lives. It was a very stressful time of discord, disappointment and unintended consequences. I needed a friend's shoulder to lean on. It was impossible for me to go far from the farm, so we basked in the river in between chores and had dinner at Buxton's main house with Dave and Dick, the farm owners. It was a relaxing delicious dinner on their back patio with views of the land, animals and lots of laughter. I really appreciated Shelley for taking time out of her busy schedule to join us at Buxton Farm. Before she left she insisted we were working too hard, and she was probably right, but focusing on that idea wouldn't get the job done, so we didn't dwell on it. We had to persevere.

My parents were slow getting around but somehow managed to find the stamina to visit us in early spring our second season. My sister Chris and her husband Roger brought them to the farm. Dad took one look at Buxton and proclaimed, "This place is a hell of a lot of work." He shook his head in disbelief at the size of the property and our responsibilities. He was also astonished we moved across the country from California to live so rurally. By this time, we were used to responses like his. Buxton's beauty was clear to us, but not to everyone who made the journey out to visit us. Dad jumped right in and helped clean thirty-five dozen eggs. Michael was impressed with his efficiency and speed.

My niece, Chelsey, and her friend Avery also came to visit our second season for a few days in late summer. Chelsey's life was academically full and soon she would be leaving for Senegal, Africa as part of a Student Exchange Program. Michael and I were thrilled we got to see her before she departed. By this time, I was acclimated to being the only female presence on the farm, but it was always a nice feeling when more women dropped in. In preparation for her trip to Africa where her vegetarian diet would consist of meat again, Chesley tried some of our pasture raised chicken and confessed it was tender and delicious.

It was wicked hot during their visit, and we didn't have the luxury of air conditioning, so after cooling off in the river with the rest of the gang at Buxton, I took them for tea and a tour of the Homestead Resort in Hot Springs. Going from the farm to that lavish resort felt like entering Disneyland. It was the closest spot we had for social contact, and although it wasn't my style, it was fun taking breaks and treating visitors to a unique and beautiful part of Bath County. Although I wasn't concerned for Chelsey's well-being like I was after her father was murdered, I knew she was still navigating her way through her life story and trying to find meaning in her life. I enjoyed checking in with her to make sure things were heading in the direction she wanted, and I always looked forward to our conversations. Like her mother, she enjoyed long esoteric discussions about the world.

Apprentices

We placed ads for apprentices on different farming sites and because we worked with Polyface we had quite a few responses. Early on in our first season we invited a group of students from Harrisonburg, Virginia to come out to Buxton. They volunteered on farms sowing seeds, harvesting, weeding and working side by side with farmers learning different skills. They were part of an organization called Crop Mobs. I was intrigued when I read about them in *Edible Blue Ridge Magazine* and I invited them out to Buxton to help us butcher our second batch of broilers. About eight of them made the long drive out to the farm and set up camp in the barn. They spent the afternoon relaxing, exploring the land, and they enjoyed a rapid ride down the Cowpasture River. The Crop Mobbers were an impressive group of students with an eagerness to learn everything about processing poultry. One student in particular made an impression on us because although she was a vegetarian, she butchered a chicken. We applauded her interest and her bravery.

Since we'd had a good experience WWOOFing in Italy, we also opened the door to WWOOFers. Extra hands were needed processing our poultry so short-term farmhands, like WWOOFers, worked perfectly. In exchange for helping us for five hours on the farm each day, we provided them room and board.

A few volunteers came from big cities and couldn't handle the solitude. We had only one cell phone service that worked in the mountains, and if they didn't have it, they were out of luck. We didn't have wireless internet. For some, it was too much of a stretch to live unplugged. One guy couldn't wait to get back on the grid, at the end of his commitment he raced back to the city. He was pleased he came for the experience, but in the end, Buxton Farm was way out of his comfort zone.

Another kid came from the South without any farm experience at all. He was sweet, with a big heart, and a great desire to learn. One day he was working out in the pasture by himself and failed to let us know a young heifer was giving birth. He assumed she would eventually deliver the calf on her own, so instead of informing us, he continued working. A few hours later, when we went to move the herd to fresh pasture, and we noticed the young heifer was distressed. When we got over to her, we saw the calf was stuck. Fortunately, Carl was on the farm that day, so I jumped on the ATV and went looking for him. After a lot of effort, he and Michael pulled the calf out of mom, but it was too late; the calf was dead. It remained a mystery to us why our volunteer chose not to inform us of her condition. Unfortunately it caused that cow a tremendous amount of unnecessary pain. Episodes like this were exactly why one of us always had to be on the farm and within reach of the animals.

One volunteer was a young man from Switzerland who was trained in the army, so hard work wasn't foreign to him. He also came from a family of farmers. He was focused, present and easy to work with. We were inspired by his family farm stories and impressed with his knowledge. I enjoyed working alongside him in our garden. He dedicated that summer to WWOOFing on farms that interested him across the U.S. We made sure he had the opportunity to visit Polyface Farm while he was with us.

We were impressed with another volunteer who rode the train all the way across the country from California. He came with an extensive permaculture background. The timing of his arrival was perfect because it was late in our first season and by then there was a defined rhythm in our schedule with chores and butchering. He fit right in at Buxton. Around that time Michael was playing music with new neighbors and homesteading friends, Don and Cathy. When Don learned our apprentice knew how to play a washboard he quickly persuaded him to join them. Before we knew it Don named their group; "better'n nothin," and they played almost every

Saturday morning at our local farmers market in Hot Springs Virginia. They were a hoot!

When people came to apprentice with us, we reveled in their stories, wishes, and dreams. Most were eager, excited, and willing to learn, and we wanted to feed their enthusiasm. Their energy made us feel the potential of the farm. Each one of them worked hard and contributed to our success in some way. Whether they butchered chickens, rescued flooding poultry, or cooked for us, we appreciated all their efforts. We considered it a privilege they wanted to come and work with us, but since so many things were new to us too, we often didn't have answers to some of the questions they asked. That was humbling.

Unfortunately that old farmhouse wasn't the best arrangement for living with people. Since it was over a hundred years old everything creaked when someone walked or moved. If an apprentice got up in the middle of the night to use the bathroom, or came in late, we woke up. Eventually the lack of sleep and privacy wore us down. By the middle of our first season, we asked apprentices and volunteers to sleep in a tent in the barn, or any place that appealed to them on the property. We simply had to get some rest. In addition, using the energy to manage people was something neither of us enjoyed, and we also weren't very good at it either. As a result, our first season we would go weeks in between volunteers simply because we needed a break. The gap between house guests gave us time to regroup, and also made us aware that living and working with people required a tremendous amount of cooperation and communication. As much as Michael and I enjoyed being social, we quickly learned we also require a fair amount of personal time and space.

Snowbirds and New Friends

We took Buxton on as an adventure and since everything was new to us our first season we were overwhelmed 90 percent of the time. Learning how to farm the land with animals was our first priority but we also got a crash course in construction, community living, and pastoral living. We juggled a lot of different hats at once, and as a result our initiation to our new lifestyle felt brutal at times. When it came time to renew our contract, we had to think long and hard about how we might make our second year better. We had long discussions about leaving and not leaving. Our salary was nothing to write home about, but getting rich wasn't why we were there.

I thought getting away in winter would restore our spirits, but it was impossible because we had our hens to take care of. Then something unexpected happened. A few weeks before the cows were scheduled to return to Swoope for winter Polyface picked up all of the remaining hens and took them home too. Without any animals tying us to the farm, we were free to do one of our favorite things: travel.

The day after the cows went back to Polyface for winter, we drove south. I still remember crossing from Georgia into Florida in December. I got out of the car at the visitor's center and the warm sunshine fell against my back. My whole body relaxed. I could hardly wait to see the ocean, get off my foot, and rest. We found a place to rent within walking distance to a beach on the Gulf of Mexico, and for the first time in our lives we were "snowbirds."

White sand beaches, sparkling, calm warm water, and amazing sunsets on the Gulf of Mexico were the perfect prescription for rejuvenation. In the evenings, after we made fresh seafood in our small cottage, we walked two blocks into town to hear live music. Early mornings, we took short walks across the white sand and looked forward to a relaxing day. We brought a variety of different books and read them in between long swims in the ocean. A few times I was fortunate enough to tread alongside dolphins. We got accustomed to the sounds of the gentle waves and after a light lunch we took short naps. Our bodies responded well to the relaxing atmosphere.

What surprised us most about being snowbirds was that after a month we were ready to go home. Our reprieve was exactly what we needed but the incredible peaceful setting Buxton emanated was hard to replicate. We drove back to Virginia totally renewed. Our long siesta contributed to our decision to commit to a second season.

Right before our first season ended, we were introduced to Bert Carlson and his wife, Marion Quinlan. As it turned out, their home overlooked Buxton Farm and during the season, they enjoyed watching us herd cattle and move poultry from a distance. Not only did they become regular customers of our pasture raised chicken and eggs, they also became good friends and neighbors. Bert's an incredibly talented musician and his band, Loose Change, played live music in Lexington, Virginia. We made a point of attending as many of his performances as possible. In the heart of winter live music was exactly what we needed to lift our spirits.

We also shared a passion for gardening and music with new friends Don and Cathy. On Tuesday nights, we ventured with them to Marino's, an old bar and restaurant in Staunton that housed some of the best musicians on that side of the state; old-timers had jammed there for over forty years. From the outside Marino's is the kind of place you would drive right past without recognizing it as a landmark, but once we learned what was going on inside that storefront, we couldn't resist the long drive there. Musicians played a variety of different instruments: banjo, harmonica, fiddle, guitar and stand up bass. The music ranged anywhere from country music to bluegrass music. We were like sardines squished together in the back room, but we loved every minute of it!. Marino's was an authentic experience.

When we learned Brendon and Susan from Stone House Farm lived one town over from us we were eager to meet them. As it turned out they apprenticed at King Hill Farm in Maine after we left. What were the odds? Brendon and Susan were replicating what they learned from Dennis King, the farmer who inspired us in Maine. They sold their vegetables at Lexington, Virginia's farmers market, and to Polyface who sold them to local restaurant accounts. Brendon's commitment to growing nutrient rich vegetables was obvious; everything tasted delicious. We truly enjoyed reminiscing with them about different adventures we had at King Hill Farm in Maine, and we also enjoyed their apple cider potluck in fall.

Going into another season with a few friends within reach strengthened our commitment to stay on at Buxton. But, every time we took a few steps away from our confined lifestyle on the farm, there was always something that pulled us back. In winter it wasn't the animals, but our source of heat. We couldn't leave the farmhouse for long because we heated only with wood. If we were gone too long, the stoves went out, and we returned to a freezing cold house, which was dreadfully uncomfortable. Getting home in time to stoke the fire became a necessity.

Neuroplasticity

Our second winter was unusually warm. In the middle of January, high temperatures were close to fifty degrees. It was bizarre, but at the same time it made winter feel more manageable. Because of my injured foot I was unable to take long hikes every day, so I took shorter walks closer to the farmhouse. Having the tiny to retreat to our second season was perfect.

Over the years of living with MCS I had stayed in touch with a few people like me, eager to find solutions for our condition. When I learned Ashok Gupta's Amygdala and Sympathetic Nervous System Retraining Program was offering some answers, I was curious and immediately bought his DVDs.

It wasn't the first time I'd come across the idea of rewiring the brain for health. About a year before we moved to Buxton Farm, I traveled to San Francisco and took Annie Hoppers workshop, "The Dynamic Neural Retraining System." Annie's premise regarding MCS is that the limbic part of the brain is impaired, and in order to create positive changes in the structure and function of it, the trauma cycle has to be consciously interrupted. One of the brilliant things about her workshop was, as soon as we walked through the door, we weren't allowed to commiserate with one another about our symptoms. Instead, we immediately had to start rewiring our brains and stop the pattern of talking negatively about MCS. At first it was extremely challenging for everyone, but it made sense. If we wanted to get better, we had to tell a new story. We were also required to read Norman Doidges book, *The Brain that Changes Itself, Stories of Personal Triumphs from the Frontiers of Brain Science*. Doidges researched the benefits of neuroplasticity and discovered the brain is a dynamic organ, one that can rewire and rearrange itself as needed. I returned home with great enthusiasm after Annie's workshop and began using her exercises to rewire my amygdala. Many positive things came out of her workshop including summoning the courage to move from California to Virginia despite living with symptoms of MCS.

According to Gupta's medical research hypothesis, MCS is a neurological condition caused by abnormalities in the unconscious part of the brain called the "amygdala." The start of the illness is often accompanied by psychological or physical stress, an acute physical illness like a virus or bacterial infection, or exposure to a toxin of some kind. As a result, the amygdala, in association with the insula (another brain structure), over stimulates the body, by learning to be hyper reactive to any symptoms detected in the body. From the time of the trigger event, the amygdala continually over stimulates the sympathetic nervous system. Since the sympathetic nervous system is the body's emergency response to threats, when it's triggered, the parasympathetic nervous system (bodily repair, detoxification, digestion, etc.) is switched off, so that energy can be diverted to the emergency. In addition, the amygdala also overstimulates the rest of the brain, keeping many circuits in a state of hyper-arousal. This adversely affects the levels of neurotransmitters in the brain, including serotonin and dopamine. Research also shows that there may also be a negative effect on the immune system, showing up as a unique pattern in each patient. As a result, the immune system is compromised. Ongoing excessive stimulation can cause symptoms that in some instances severely affect every single organ and system in the body, including the endocrine (hormonal) system. The continual stimulation can also cause secondary effects in the body such as allergies. This has led researchers to think that those effects are the cause of the condition, when really they are simply symptoms of a deeper underlying brain abnormality.

The frustration that comes living with MCS can be extreme at times. Primarily because once symptoms like brain fog, or migraines get activated, there's no recourse for stopping them, and typically, as Gupta explained, they trigger other symptoms. It becomes a domino affect, often resulting in feelings of frustration, despair and hopelessness. In truth, I appreciated my body for alerting me to toxic environments, but a constant state of vigilance isn't my description for a healthy life.

Gupta's DVD's helped me better understand why all the alternative therapies I tried in an effort to cure myself of MCS had failed. As I continued to grasp the implications of his research, I realized MCS is comparative to people living with brain injuries. Not always as extreme, but the damage to the limbic system, in my opinion, is certainly similar. My amygdala was in a constant state of post-traumatic stress. If rewiring my limbic system would allow me to live like a normal person, capable of being inside our farmhouse and in buildings like our local library or friends' homes in winter without reacting then I was in. Gupta's research was another answered prayer.

I liked Gupta's style, confidence and commitment. His own personal story of living with chronic fatigue gave him a solid understanding of persistent illness. I immediately started doing his guided meditations, positive visualizations and awareness exercises.

After three months of studying his DVD's and implementing his exercises into my daily life, I felt a tremendous amount of hope and clarity. I learned the value of slowing down my thoughts and my reactions, and I felt deeply empowered doing the visualizations. Once spring arrived and our season started, I was outside in my element again, the one place where I'm unguarded. With the season in full swing I didn't have as much free time for his DVD's, but everyday I committed to his guided meditations.

"2012 Allies; Alec on left and Trevor on right"

Second Season Allies and Savoring

In January 2011, we were being contacted by young people about apprenticing on the farm for our second season. We learned a lot our first season and so we were clear on what we did and did not want when it came to apprentices. In fact, our second season we weren't looking for just apprentices but allies, people we knew we could count on no matter what. Fortunately, Joel and Daniel gave us a list of guidelines they had implemented for their apprentices and interns, and we modified it to fit Buxton. It gave apprentices an idea of what was expected of them and vice versa. We tried to be very specific with the guidelines, and although we didn't expect anyone to be perfect, we knew we didn't want smokers, drinkers, or vegetarians. There was no time to deal with special diets or personal addictions, and because we had to butcher four thousand meat birds, we knew the farm wasn't the right place for anyone with an aversion to meat. We started at sunrise and sometimes weren't finished until sunset; it was vital for apprentices to keep up with us. We gave weekends off, so they had plenty of time to explore exquisite Virginia. Thus, it was imperative for them to have their own transportation.

It was a delicate balance to use the farmhouse as a business and a home, and we valued our privacy, so we were very upfront about keeping our part of the house separate. Michael and I had the downstairs bathroom, along with our office, and the tiny studio for our sleeping space. The second floor of the farmhouse was for apprentices, and the kitchen and dining room were communal. I requested no strong scents like cologne, perfume, incense or strong laundry detergents be used in the house. We paid them a monthly stipend and provided all meals, including a delicious dinner that we prepared every night of the week. Clear communication was encouraged, in an effort to keep us from having to read minds. If someone had an issue we wanted to know what it was and what we could do to improve the situation, even if it meant cutting our losses and moving on. Rules could be easily modified if we got the right people, to suit them and us. The guidelines were extremely helpful as we prepared for our second season. We wanted the experience to be a win-win for everyone.

It was essential to spend time with prospective apprentices before inviting them to live and work with us for a season. Polyface calls it a "check out" visit and it's standard procedure for all their applicants. More than anything, it helps weed out people who are willing to apprentice but aren't necessarily the right match.

We invited Alec from Charlottesville, Virginia, to our first check out. Alec loved nature and was totally comfortable working outside. He was considerate, lighthearted, funny, caring, in great physical shape and had construction experience. His desire to learn the Polyface model of farming was born long before Joel leased farms like Buxton. Alec visited Polyface when he was in grade school, and was interested in apprenticing because he intended to rent land near his home and farm on a small scale. Being from Charlottesville gave him the opportunity to live and work with us during the week and go home on weekends. He was a perfect match, so we invited him to join us for our second season. He jumped right in with the details of the herd, poultry chores and butchering. He came with a lot of great ideas so Michael and I learned a lot from him. Together the three of us established a great system.

In mid-June, a young man from Georgia contacted us with the hopes of joining as our second apprentice. He had read a lot about Polyface Farms and was eager to gain experience with pasture-raised livestock. Trevor was lighthearted, confident, happy, and motivated. We were won over by his insistence on coming to Buxton, and invited him to join our team in early July. He arrived a few days after the derecho hit, and was blown away by the damage.

Trevor immediately fit in at Buxton because he was extremely independent. During his weekends off he camped, hiked and explored Virginia on his own. He had a quick pace and got chores done in record time. His stories about working in small villages in South America entertained all of us. He was fearless, positive, and introduced us to many new things. His sense of humor was always in evidence; every day he had us laughing about something. In the short time we knew Trevor, we watched him accomplish everything he put his heart and mind into. Michael and I enjoyed watching him expand his knowledge as he gained hands-on experience at Buxton. He brought a lot of joy to the farm. He and Alec, our other apprentice, became friends and the four of us made a great team.

Late that summer we invited two additional short term volunteers to come and work with us. By then the external effects of the derecho had diminished, and we had a defined momentum on the farm again. The hardest part for all of our volunteers was waking at dawn. A lot of them just weren't morning people. It took a little time for them to get up to speed with us and morning chores, but for Michael and I, early morning was the best part of the day.

One volunteer was a young woman from Louisiana. She was a culinary student who planned on raising her own food for her family and possibly one day owning a restaurant. I loved being in a position to inspire volunteers to follow their hearts. She had great stamina, was a fast learner, was unafraid to butcher chickens, and she knew sweating is good for the soul. Her sweet Southern ways grew on us. Her first few nights in the farmhouse were a little nerve wracking because we slept with unlocked doors, windows open, and we left keys in all of our vehicles. We didn't think anything of it, but where she came from this kind of nonchalant attitude was unthinkable.

We appreciated the variety of young people and the individual intentions they brought to Buxton Farm; each of them were unique. We kept Joel's books on hand for interns to read during their visit because seeing things firsthand and then reading his books were the perfect combination to spark their personal farming desires.

The last guy who came to work with us contacted us after hiking the Appalachian Trail. He was an agricultural student from up north and he was interested in Polyface's model of pasture-raised farming. His energy was entirely different from anyone we had worked with yet that season. He was more serious, moved slower, and was a deep thinker. His favorite part of the farm was working with the herd. We knew he was being taught the conventional way to farm in school, so we were glad he took the time to see the results with intensive-grazing cows. He was impressed with the outcome.

Farming, homesteading, and gardening appeal to Michael and me because we love food! Nourishing food: food grown and cooked with love and appreciation. Every evening, we prepared dinner for our apprentices, so meal prep was also on our list of things to do. Being fans of Sally Fallon recipes, we slow cooked as many meals as possible. Sandor Katz's book, *Wild Fermentation, The Flavor, Nutrition, and Craft of Live-Culture Foods,* also came in handy for homemade ginger brews, sauerkraut, bread, and other fermented goodies. Teresa Salatin shared her homemade granola recipe with me and I made it every week. Our apprentice Trevor loved it so much he couldn't start the day without it, so he took over the responsibility of preparing it every week our second season. Pasture-raised pork became one of our favorite dishes. The taste was supreme over what we were accustomed to in California. In fact, it reminded us of the delicious pork we ate at King Hill Farm in Maine. Often we started the day with pork sausage, eggs and vegetables. Because we were constantly active, eating protein was essential. Physically demanding work and good protein sources went hand and hand. Being subcontractors for Polyface, we received a discount at their farm store and since we enjoyed eating a fair amount of protein, that savings came in handy.

One volunteer came from New York City said he had never eaten so well in his life! Between the grass-fed meat, poultry, and pork, and the raw milk and homemade yogurt, he was in foodie heaven. Another apprentice grew up with a vegetarian influence, and he claimed he ate more meat the two months he lived and worked with us then he had his entire life! He was certainly free to eat whatever he wished but for most of us carbohydrates didn't sustain us. I don't think I was the only one who learned how to savor food in a new way. After working hard all day everything seemed to taste better.

In California drinking a beer from time to time didn't really appeal to me, but in Virginia it was a different story. The hard work and humid atmosphere were the best combination for enjoying a cold beer occasionally, and who couldn't use additional B vitamins? After Pierre, our french friend, Permaculture master and beer connoisseur introduced us to the incredible local beer choices in Nelson County, Virginia, we couldn't resist indulging in a cold one after a long day on the farm. The taste was supreme.

I had fond memories of picking wild black raspberries for my Grandma in Ohio when I was a teenager. It was such a pleasure to find these delicious berries were abundant at Buxton Farm. In between chores, two of us would spend an hour or two a day harvesting them. It wasn't easy, but we wore heavy clothes and endured the thorns and heat because they were so delicious. They were everywhere we looked our second season. Trevor and Alec spent several weeks helping us harvest them. They were good sports! I rewarded their efforts with homemade black raspberry crumbles for dessert, and jam for homemade pancakes and bread. We froze remaining berries and then, along with our homemade yogurt, added them to fruit smoothies. In the end, one thing was certain: at Buxton Farm we ate like kings.

Honey Bees And Guardian Geese

Once I established a rhythm on our homestead in Santa Ynez with growing vegetables and butchering our poultry, I took a beekeeping class in Santa Barbara with master beekeeper Don from San Marcos Farm. At first the bees intimidated me, but then the closer I got to observing them, the more they fascinated me. I was impressed with how delicately the queen bee quietly runs the show. Her communal commitment activated a deep respect within me for the colony. My intention as a beekeeper was to do my part to help them thrive.

Immediately following the bee course, I drove to Los Angeles and bought my first Langstroth Beehive, along with additional equipment and a suit for protection. I put the beehive in the yard where I could see it everyday so that I could envision bees finding it. It sat empty for several months. Then, one day, a swarm flew inside a hole in our neighbors oak tree. I was overjoyed, but I had no idea how I would catch them. Fortunately Santa Barbara's Master Beekeeper, Don, came over and showed me how to drive the bees out of the tree using smoke. I spent the next three days traveling up and down a very steep ladder onto our neighbor's roof. It was dangerous and it took time, but eventually I lured the bees in their new home and then Michael and I moved them next door to our homestead. Catching that swarm was an intense initiation into beekeeping, but the reward of having my first hive made all of it well worth it!

At Buxton I waited a year before adding any new animals to the farm and since I was still a new beekeeper, I didn't want to lose what I learned in California about beekeeping. In early spring our second season I drove up to Highland County near West Virginia and bought bees from a woman with eight hives. Since there weren't any large conventional farms near us, Buxton was a sanctuary for honeybees; they flourished in our pristine environment.

I was fortunate to participate in a beekeeping class out first season with Gunther Hauk, founder of Spikenard Farm and Honeybee Sanctuary in Floyd, Virginia. Gunther recommends feeding bees only when it's absolutely necessary and his recipe includes herbs, with honey as the sweetener rather than white sugar. Incidentally, whenever I prepared that recipe I made enough for me. It's a healthy delicious tonic.

Michael and Alec were setting fence lines up for the herd's next move when they discovered a nest of honeybees inside the water wellspring. I was stunned when they told me about them because I saw them swarm from our original hive a few weeks earlier and I wondered where they went. I didn't enjoy interrupting their new quarters, but they were in direct competition with the cows for space. Being close to the ground, the herd would eventually obliterate the hive. Alec was eager to learn about bees, so together we carefully cut the comb and moved them back to the farmhouse into one of our Langstroth hives. We were absolutely amazed at how beautifully designed their honeycomb was inside that wellspring. They were a particularly docile hive, and so working intimately with them was effortless.

My next addition to the farm was a pair of geese. I found them advertised on craigslist. Alec picked them up for me on his way back to Buxton from Charlottesville. The owners claimed geese were excellent poultry guardians. Apparently one of their geese fight off a bobcat attack. I was impressed and I was hoping the geese might make good guardians for our hens, but Alec and I quickly discovered they preferred living with the turkeys instead. Anytime a hawk or eagle made its way to the turkeys, the geese would honk, and our flock of turkeys would run for cover under their shade mobile. The geese were two handsome males. I named them Nelson and Mandela. They had a great life on fresh pasture, rain, sunshine and lots of friends. I will never forget when Polyface picked up the turkeys for processing later in the season. The geese looked lost without their buddies.

Mishaps and Hospital Visits

Before we knew it our first season arrived and the cows were scheduled to return to Buxton. Before they did I decided to get a head start on our kitchen garden. We were putting up our pea trellis one cold, windy, spring morning our first season when the knife on Michael's Leatherman went straight into the side of his leg. He was cutting twine for the trellis, when the blade slipped. We hustled inside, bandaged his leg, and drove to the emergency room, where a surgeon put in a few stitches. Although the injury wasn't severe, anything that interfered with his responsibility for the herd weighed heavily on his mind. There really wasn't time to deal with injuries or accidents at Buxton, we had a lot on our plate and since Daniel Salatin and his team of apprentices were an hour away, it came down to just me and Michael. Fortunately, he was back to normal in just a couple of days.

In April 2011 our first season was just getting started, and my foot was in a lot of pain. Working with an injury was terribly frustrating. I iced it after chores, but I was concerned because the pain was sharp and no matter what I tried, it wouldn't go away. As much as I don't like hospitals, I decided it was time for some answers. After seeing the x-ray, the local podiatrist suggested surgery. I was shocked and thought his solution was a bit extreme, and because of my history with surgeons there was no way I was going to let this young podiatrist cut into my foot. I thanked him for his time, and looked forward to getting a second opinion once the season was over. When the pain continued a few weeks later, I requested from the same doctor who referred me to the podiatrist, a physical therapist and I was so pleased to find one within reach of Buxton. Unfortunately, I didn't have time for those appointments until the season was nearly over.

In addition to injuries, at some point during the high season our first year, I noticed a nodule in one breast; every once in awhile it ached. Since the tumor and surgery on my left leg, I didn't taking chances with unusual growths of any kind, so I immediately scheduled an appointment with a specialist at Bath County Hospital.

A compassionate nurse walked me through the details of my appointment. I felt vulnerable and knew my life could change in a heartbeat if the test results indicated unhealthy cells. During the examination and testing, I was distracted with dark thoughts of a forbidding future, but I immediately cast those negative thoughts to the side, and steadied my breath and my anxious thoughts. Sitting quietly in meditation, I waited for the results. During that short contemplation I reflected on how rich my life with Michael was and how much I loved what we were doing. Our commitment to follow our bliss brought us all the way to rural Virginia to farm with Polyface. I proclaimed to the universe, "I'm not going anywhere." Deep within, I was almost certain it was a cyst, and thankfully, I was proven right. I sailed back to Buxton elated and in awe of our demanding but vibrant life on the farm. The good news restored my commitment to healthy living once again.

In California, summer squash grows quickly and easily, but successfully raising it in Virginia was challenging. We enjoyed cooking baby squash with eggs for breakfast, but our second season the squash vine borer bug was a nightmare. As a result, I spent a fair amount of time in the garden every morning eliminating as many squash bugs as possible, and since I enjoy putting my bare hands into the soil to look for worms, I often left the garden with dirty soil stained hands. One morning some soil got wedged under my thumb. I tried getting it out but a few particles remained and before I knew it, my thumb was sore throbbed through the night. I tried healing it with hydrogen peroxide, Epsom salt soaks, and a few other home remedies, but nothing worked. It was infected.

Back at Bath County Hospital, the emergency doctor punctured the infected area and drained the pus without a local anesthetic. The pain was so intense, I thought I might pass out. Fortunately, a strong and fearless nurse gave me permission to squeeze her hand during the process. The pain took me back to my childhood days when I resisted Novocain at the dentist. Being a tomboy, I insisted I could handle the pain. Back then my motto was: "No pain, no gain." What was I thinking? Nonetheless, that old warrior-like attitude came in handy more than once at Buxton. We learned pretty quickly farming land and shepherding animals required a certain amount of resiliency. I'm not sure what we would have done without Bath County Hospital right over the mountain from us, but I was ready for that to be my last visit—they were starting to know me.

Michael was securing the fence line along the forest one afternoon when he hit a bush with a hive of wild bees inside. They swarmed around him, stung his face, his backside, and his head. The following day, he looked like he'd been in a fist fight; his right eye was swollen and bruised.

All sorts of mishaps occurred working that land. Whether it was overpowering weather patterns, running from lightning in the open pasture, crossing flooding rivers, or cutting ourselves while processing our chickens, we never knew what to expect.

One time, we were working with the herd and our drunken neighbor plowed through a fence line and demanded we get in his truck. His aggressive behavior startled me. When we realized he was drunk, we asked him to leave the property and not return. His carelessness could have created a nightmare for us if the herd had discovered the broken fence line.

"Eggmobile and laying hens at dawn"

Pioneers and Predators

When I took my first Permaculture Design Course (PDC), Darren Doherty, a Permaculture Teacher from Australia, taught the first half of it. His body of work about restoring land made an lasting impression on me. I was a student of his for a short but insightful time and I never really expected our paths would cross again, but as it turned out after Joel taught The Carbon Economy Series in Santa Barbara, California, Joel and Darren became good friends

Darren, his wife Lisa, and their beautiful creative children came to Virginia our first summer to film a documentary about Polyface Farms. We were thrilled they made the journey out to our pristine environment at Buxton. They filmed the herd, took a plunge in the crystal clear river, and before they left, interviewed Michael and me.

Lisa asked how studying permaculture had influenced our decision to team up with Polyface. It was a good question. Since taking Darren's permaculture design course, I knew I wanted to be involved with sustainable living practices on some level. I also knew a lifestyle of working the land, pasture-raising animals and immersing myself in nature were key ingredients to making me stronger and improving my vitality. It's been said, "If you have your health, you have everything." Ever since my health was compromised, I've followed every impulse to increase my longevity. When the opportunity came to integrate my knowledge of Permaculture principles with farming, it felt like a win-win opportunity.

Every summer, Sally Fallon Morell, a pioneer in the slow food movement, participates in The Farm-to-Consumer Legal Defense Fund fundraiser at

Polyface. The Farm to Legal Defense Fund is a grassroots organization that protects the rights of the nation's family farms, artisan food producers, consumers and affiliate communities to engage in direct commerce, free of harassment by federal, state and local government interference. Joel is a founding member of the FTCLDF and affectionately refers to them as "The Food NRA." Sally's cookbook, *Nourishing Traditions, The Cookbook that Challenges Politically Correct Nutrition and the Diet Dictocrats,* was a key ingredient in restoring my health after cancer. After a decade of using her recipes I was thrilled when Teresa Salatin introduced me to her.

President of the Weston A. Price Foundation, and founder of "A Campaign for Real Milk," Sally is the leading spokesperson for nutrient-dense diets including raw milk, animal fats, organ meats, bone broths and lacto-fermented foods. I embraced her recommendations for soaking nuts and flours, making fermented drinks, increasing healthy fats, and eating pasture-raised meat and poultry. As a result, my digestion and stamina improved dramatically. I carried her cookbook twice across the country from Maine to California, and California to Virginia. Rarely did a week go by that I didn't refer to one of her recipes. Thanks to her sharing the findings of Dr. Weston A. Price, I understood the relationship between diet, health, and nutritional deficiencies as factors for good dental health. Price was a Cleveland dentist who traveled to isolated parts of the globe to study the health of populations untouched by Western civilization. When he observed that non-industrialized people were virtually free of physical degeneration and tooth decay, he realized that beautiful straight teeth and strong bodies were typical of primitives who ate traditional diets rich in essential food factors. Fallon's dedication to restoring nutrient-dense food to our diet through research, education, and activism certainly changed my eating habits, and ultimately my lifestyle. She has been one of my strongest influences.

As fate would have it, Wendell Berry, food activist, farmer and writer, came to Virginia one summer evening. The Virginia Horse Center Foundation in Lexington held timed horse pull competitions, and working horses are one of Berry's passions. Lexington's "Chicken Whisperer" Pat Foreman told us about the competition, so I went and took an apprentice from California and a volunteer who came out from the city with me. Joel, Teresa, Joel's mom, Lucille, and Polyface interns and apprentices attended as well.

It was my first time at a timed horse pull competition, and although it's not my thing, the horses were impressive. Before the event started, Joel introduced all of us to Wendell Berry. We were all fans. I grew up across the river from him in Ohio but was unaware of this prolific writer, educator, activist, and farmer until we worked on the farm in Maine. Berry was another person who inspired my desire to practice sustainable principles and raise local food. He spoke immediately after the horse competition and shared some of his personal insights about farming, politics and his farm in Kentucky. I was pleased we had the opportunity to share a brief but informative evening with him.

In our second season we started out much more relaxed, but then in late June the derecho hit, and shortly after that nightmare, we had two unexpected predator attacks. At dawn, one morning I heard a dog barking out by the river. It was common for us to have dogs chase wildlife on the other side of the river, so I didn't think too much of it until I remembered Jack wasn't guarding the broilers or turkeys. The hens were a few miles down the road from the farm, and being so far away from us, I thought they were more vulnerable, so the night before I put Jack with them instead.

Michael and I were in the mudroom dressing for morning chores when I noticed a hound dog by our kitchen garden. By the time we stepped outside, he was gone. As we approached the broiler pasture, we saw our turkeys scattered all over the field, not one was eaten, but they all had broken necks. A few still had some life in them, but the remaining seventy were dead. I wanted to scream, but instead I started to cry. Since turkeys are delicate and harder to raise than broilers, I had spent six weeks nurturing that group. Everyday I supplemented their diet with yogurt, hard-boiled eggs, and warmer brooder temperatures. I was thrilled all of them were strong when we put them out to pasture.

From what we could tell, the dog ripped through the chicken wire, and then dug beneath each pen to get to them. We knew it was the hound dog because the turkeys weren't eaten; he killed out of instinct. It was agonizing to see so much precious life wasted. With tears in our eyes, we picked up each carcass and put them in the compost pile. It was a good thing the dog wasn't there when we arrived because the outrage I felt was irrepressible. I finally understood the importance of owning a gun. As much as I hated to admit it, I could have shot that dog for killing our turkeys. Losing that many turkeys was a huge financial loss for us and for Polyface.

The welfare of our animals was always on our minds so when things like predator attacks happened on our watch, it took a lot of self restraint not to berate ourselves when things didn't work out exactly as we intended. It was hard to accept, but the reality was, it never would have happened if we hadn't removed Jack from guarding them the night before.

What I gained from this experience was that Buxton Farm ultimately needed two guard dogs. Three hundred acres spread out across a farm the size of Buxton, was too much area to cover for only one. From that day forward, Jack didn't leave the turkeys and broiler pens. The hens were on their own.

Michael, Alec, Trevor and I took turns closing up the hens each night before dark. We discovered our second massacre of the season when Michael and I went out one morning to open up the eggmobile and chicken body parts were scattered around the field. One of our apprentices forgot to close up the laying hens in their eggmobile. Without Jack to protect them, it was a free-for-all for predators. Hens left behind were in shock, they stood there in a trance dazed and confused. It was hard to swallow after our turkey losses, and since we couldn't pull Jack from our broilers or turkeys, I decided I would sleep in our car with a gun and wait for the predator to return. I didn't sleep a wink that night, and I was relieved I didn't have to use the gun. Other than a raccoon that I chased off, the night was quiet. The raccoon came back the next night and walked right into a trap Michael had waiting for him. It was another financial loss for us to lose that many hens because their eggs were part of our paycheck, but what disturbed me more than losing money was the feeling that once again we let our animals down.

Our neighbor managed a rather large alpaca farm and one evening she spotted a large coyote stalking her baby alpacas. The coyote came back several nights in a row, so she invited some hunters to set up camp and wait for it to return. Unbeknownst to us, in broad daylight the next day, Jack, our guard dog, chased the coyote away from Buxton towards the alpaca farm. It just so happened those hunters were standing by that afternoon, and as the story goes, Jack cornered the coyote and a hunter shot it. Jack became a local hero. The alpaca farm manager begged for permission to adopt him, but her words fell on deaf ears because Jack was my boy.

At the risk of sounding contradictory, I personally would have considered other solutions before killing the coyote. Unlike the domesticated hound dog that killed our turkeys, the coyote hadn't done anything to render being shot. In fact, the mere presence of him was, in my opinion, more of a "fair warning" than anything else, one I would have taken to heart. Whether we liked it or not, one thing we learned about farming; predators were a constant rural reminder that we were all in this together.

External and Internal Landscapes

When our apprentice Alec brought his kayak out to Buxton, I was the first person in it! I took full advantage of living on the CowPasture River, and whenever I had a free hour, I kayaked. Easing my way down the crystal-clear river like an explorer, I witnessed wildlife at every bend, pausing to watch raccoon families, great horned owls, eagles, big fish, little fish, turtles, wild turkeys, fox, wild ducks, snakes of all shapes and sizes, and enormous bucks as they played or sipped water from the river. The river had immense healing qualities and kayaking it was not only soothing, but also a great source of entertainment.

At one specific turn in the river was a sacred spot of land, an old cemetery. Stones were placed in a circle to mark graves, clearly defining where souls were buried, reminders of stories from the past. The stones had been there a long time, but the landowners weren't certain if the graves represented slaves or Native Americans. There was a tremendous amount of history on Buxton Farm. Whoever chose that spot to bury loved ones knew something about nature, the elements, and a bigger perspective. It wasn't a random choice. The vibration in that spot was very strong, almost like a current, or vortex of energy. It was a sacred spot. I sensed it every time I visited and I felt privileged to know it existed.

Right around Thanksgiving is the beginning of hunting season, and the deer know it. I don't know where they go, but a lot of them suddenly disappear. Kip and her brothers seldom visited Buxton during this time of the year. The energy of the farm changes dramatically. For about six weeks I had to minimize walks in the woods, cover myself in orange, dodge hunters on the property and acclimate to the continuous sound of gun shots echoing throughout the forest. It was slightly unnerving at times. Old-timers had hunted on Buxton property for decades. I thought for certain I would want to hunt for deer with them when we first moved to Buxton Farm. But when I saw how many hours were involved sitting still in freezing cold temperatures, I quickly lost all interest. We did however, enjoy slow cooked deer meat. Thanks to Daniel Salatin we learned how to gut deer at Polyface our first season.

I was out on an early Sunday morning walk and found a deer tangled in a fence. Her hoof was caught and she was hanging by one leg. I raced home, got Michael, grabbed a pair of pliers, and we drove back to free her. When we got close, she grew terrified. I talked softy to her while Michael cut the wire out of her hoof. As soon as her leg dropped she tried to run, but was in bad shape. I realized she might not last long, but I thought I owed it to her to let her run free one final time. After she realized the condition of her wound, she looked back at us before she limped off into the forest. Unfortunately it wasn't the first time I saw a dead deer hanging on a fence at Buxton Farm.

In summer Bath Country Car Collision stayed in business because of an increase in deer-related accidents. It seemed like everyone we knew hit a deer at least once that season. Driving country roads, especially at night, was a risk; the deer were everywhere. They bounded out from the forest, ran across the road, or hugged the side of it, and then sometimes darted in front of us. One evening Michael, Alec, and Trevor and I went into town to hear Bert Carlson's band, Loose Change. On our drive home I was a nervous wreck because it was dark, and we came closing to hitting a deer. I was constantly reminded of my sister Kim's deer related fatal automobile accident. In order for us to miss them, we had to move at a snail's pace. If we went out for dinner or to hear music, we tried getting home before it got dark. It was another constraint in our social life and often kept us on the farm during the season.

During the first season our pastures were affected by drought. Unlike other states, we weren't desperate for water, but we watched grass dry up to the point where the number of cow grazing days was reduced. Much to our surprise, Joel and Daniel had us feed hay for a few weeks in August to give the pastures time to catch up. It worked.

One morning, I was driving our farm truck to the herd a few miles down the road, with Michael and Jack, our guard dog in the back. In the blink of an eye a mountain lion jumped across the road in front of us. It was rather large, moved quick as lightning, and startled me. It had been years since Carl had seen one on the property. I was certain we had the rare opportunity to see that magnificent beast simply because it came down the mountain for a drink. Fortunately, Jack didn't catch a glimpse of him. I'm not sure what would have happened if he had. When we lived on the West Coast I often hiked in the back country and would have loved to have crossed paths with one, but never did. It was a rare sighting, even in Virginia. The last thing I wanted was for hunters to go looking for him, so I kept that secret to myself.

Another afternoon we were moving the herd a few miles down the road, into a pasture adjacent to the river, when a piercing cry stopped all of us in our tracks. I thought for sure one of the cows had dropped a calf. The cry got louder and louder as more of the herd entered the pasture. I figured out the sound was coming from the cedar trees, so I ran underneath and discovered a terrified baby fawn. The cows touched her with their noses, licked her, and almost trampled her. She was only a day old. I gathered her up into my arms and looked around for mom. It was remarkable to hold such a small, wild, and extremely vulnerable creature. She smelled sweet and her body was lukewarm. I had to make a conscious effort not to get attached to her. I assumed mom bolted when she saw the herd coming but I had every intention of returning fawn to mom. I couldn't put the fawn back because she didn't stand a chance being in the same pasture as the herd, so we drove to Carl and Norma's house to ask their advice. Norma had raised motherless fawns more than once in her life, and she suggested I put the fawn outside the gate of the pasture where I found her. It was good advice, even though I was worried the fawn might be too close to the road. As soon as we got back to the pasture and out of our truck, the fawn jumped out of my arms and took cover under a bush adjacent to the gate. I was impressed she knew exactly where to go to protect herself.

My instincts said everything would work out, but I could hardly sleep that night. The next morning, I raced out at dawn, and she was gone. Later that week, we saw her and mom grazing in a nearby pasture. It was moments like this I lived for on the farm.

One afternoon I went out by myself for a short swim when I suddenly felt the presence of someone. Rocks tumbled down the cliff and splashed in the water behind me. For a minute I felt shy and modest so I hesitated before turning around. When I finally did, I discovered a river otter swimming within feet of me. I was ecstatic. I didn't want to frighten him, so I didn't stare, for fear of sending him away but inside, I was bubbling with joy. The otter stayed in its own circle for quite awhile. We each bobbed our heads in and out of the water as we enjoyed our swim. I was touched he felt safe in my presence. I'd heard stories from Carl about trapping otters on that river, and I'm glad it's now illegal. After awhile, he headed north up the river. I watched his sweet head gently bob in and out of the water as he swam away. I never saw him again.

Because we were up every day at dawn, we witnessed all sorts of wildlife. On more than one occasion we came into contact with colossal Great Horned Owls hunting prey on the driveway. Their yellow-eyed stares were intimidating. We tried to avoid coming between them and their hunt for food. It wasn't unusual to hear their territorial soft hoots throughout the night. I welcomed these songs.

We simply never knew what might reveal itself on that land. But that was what I loved about Buxton Farm. It was primitive, unpredictable, and magnificent. It had a wildness that made my heart soar. Rarely did I feel alone in those pastures and forest, it always felt like something somewhere was watching us.

Joel was on his way to teach a workshop in late summer when he called to let us know he and Daniel decided not to renew Buxton's lease at the end of the season. We weren't entirely surprised by Joel's decision, and in some ways we saw it coming. Having a satellite farm an hour away from Swoope wasn't the most practical arrangement. After five years of leasing Buxton Farm, Joel and Daniel decided to rent land closer to home.

As for us, in June after the derecho hit, Buxton Farm no longer felt like our home. We decided then that season would be our last. Nonetheless, leaving that lifestyle and land wasn't going to be easy for me. We were the only two people living full time on those thousand acres and as a result; I now felt viscerally connected to it. It was a nature lovers' paradise and I cherished it. Even though the growing season was packed with the challenges of physical work, hot days, never ending lists, and sore bodies, the hectic pace also had its rewards. During the high season the farm and the land came alive. Watching wildlife and our animals enjoy a bountiful harvest was immensely rewarding. We were in harmony with the animals we shepherded and even though we claimed none them as our own, we loved them and treated all of them as if they were.

Outside the farm it seemed like the whole world was speeding up, but internally I was slowing down. I still didn't need a cell phone, and because of our remote location, I made minimal social engagements. I grew more and more self-reflective, falling into my own internal rhythm on that magnificent land. I rose with the sun and went to sleep with the moon and stars. It got to the point where the quiet setting almost felt addictive. Without realizing it, I was learning to be comfortable and fully at peace within. Some people might compare this state of mind as "being in the zone." I always knew this feeling of invincibility existed. Ever since I left Ms. B.'s third grade classroom in Catholic school I searched for it. I looked for it in teachers, gurus, mentors, classes, food, exercise, drugs, and relationships, only to realize this unspoiled place was within. Everything I lived prior to Buxton Farm prepared me to cross this threshold of fully coming home. Wherever we went next I was certain this feeling would go with me.

Moving on

After we harvested all of our poultry, the transition from an intense-schedule to a less structured time also meant a new season is just around the corner. As soon as the leaves were at their peak, I drove to Ohio to see my parents. Living within driving distance to them at this stage in their lives was important to me. My trip to Ohio was short but very significant.

Dad was frustrated with his lack of vitality. He went from being energetic and healthy, to weak and immobile in a short amount of time. His health was questionable. Doctors weren't entirely sure what was wrong with him. I was looking forward to seeing him. The drive through the two Virginias to the Midwest is phenomenal. Spring has always been my favorite time of the year, but living in a climate with distinct seasons again made me cherish fall too.

Dad was bed bound for the first time in his life, and he wasn't happy about it. His vulnerable state reminded me of a dependent child. Mom had to feed him and care for him. He slept a lot, but in between his naps I would sit with him and tell him different stories about life on the farm. Throughout the season I wrote letters to him updating him on our most current events happening at Buxton. He was amazed at how much we enjoyed farming. We still didn't see eye to eye on on a multitude of different issues, but we no longer let our differences dictate our deeper feelings for one another.

Hi Dad   9-03-2012

I'm sitting on the side of the road, near The Homestead Resort selling our amazing tomatoes. I left a basket of them for you and mom. I hope you enjoy them as much as we do! We have so many. Just pure abundance when it comes to tomatoes. Growing them inside a hoop house has been awesome. Customers return every week with reports of how delicious they taste! It's exciting to share our abundance. I enjoy talking to people about good food!

It was so good spending time with you and trimming your hair! I'm glad you're resting and taking it easy. Mom really enjoys taking care of you, but having a nurse to assist her is a blessing.

I had a beautiful drive home to Virginia. A full moon rose high as I came over the mountains into West Virginia. It was a spectacular sight to see. It seemed so incredibly full and expansive. It took my breath away. The drive was smooth with very little traffic. But hot! So hot. I rarely use air conditioning but I had to turn it on. I simply had to cool down.

I came home to a busy farm as you know. We moved the cows down the road a few miles and that's an all day event. Fortunately Michael has it down to an art. It's hard for me to accept we will be moving on from Buxton. I will miss this lifestyle. I'm really going to miss working outdoors and being with the animals.

Tomorrow we're going on a farm tour. We hope to visit at least five small family farms. One farm raises ducks, which is something we're interested in seeing. There are so many wonderful diversified farms in Virginia. I'm so happy we're taking the time to see a few of them before we leave Buxton.

I'm not sure if I told you, but I'm seeing a second physical therapist for my foot and he has some solid but different advice *than the first physical therapist. I'm committed to the exercises he recommends and I can't wait to dance again soon!*

I know you're worried about your health but I want to encourage you to relax. Let your mind and body rest. I look forward to seeing you again soon.

Luv u

Grace

When Polyface started reclaiming the herd, I moved closer to the reality that Polyface at Buxton Farm was coming to an end. Every week, something new was dismantled. After the herd, the hoop house came down, then the broiler pens, ATV, tractor, and Jack the guard dog were trucked back to Swoope, Virginia. Without the animals, Buxton felt vacant. We didn't have any definite plans for our future, so once again we decided to sell almost everything we owned.

After two yard sales, I gave away the rest of our furniture. Our two favorite chairs went to a young couple managing another satellite farm, the twin beds used by apprentices went to Carl and Norma's grandchildren, along with a large wooden coffee table and a few other things that came with us from California. I gave away muck boots that were in perfect condition but had ruined my right foot, and sold our guard geese, Nelson and Mandela, to a family in West Virginia who had a pond. We put items we couldn't part with in a small storage space for winter, and moved our bees to a friends house nearby. Our friend Don moved our tiny portable studio away from its spot near the soothing river, the place that captured the magic of Buxton. I wondered if the pair of eagles would notice we were gone. Letting go of possessions wasn't challenging, but the thought of leaving the land was excruciating.

I was in kindergarten when I got my first pet, a beagle puppy named Penny. I don't recall who brought her home but I loved that little dog with all my heart. We were living with Grandma while our new home was being built and Grandma didn't like animals. When I came home from school one afternoon, Penny was gone. No one would tell me where she went, but I knew they took her to the shelter. My heart was broken. I cried for days and I never forgot the traumatic feelings associated with losing a pet.

Leaving the cats behind weighed heavily on my mind. We won them over with our trust and since we couldn't take them with us, I felt like we were abandoning them. Budhi, Gussy, and Tenny had become an integral part of the joy we shared almost every day on the farm. Much to my surprise, I fell in love with their distinct personalities. When we first arrived at Buxton, Budhi was the first one to let us touch him, he had absolutely no fear. It took Tennessee a couple weeks before he could get close to us, but when he finally did, he rarely let us out of his sight again. Gussy was initially terrified of us, but by the end of our first season, he finally let us in too. He became surprisingly affectionate. In winter, the three of them lived in the crawl space under the farmhouse near the wood burning stove. Whenever I ran a hot bath, their purring sounds echoed throughout my bathroom.

I didn't think Tennessee would make it without us, and because we hadn't chosen our next home yet, we couldn't take him with us. Every morning he waited patiently at the back door for us before we set out for our chores. I couldn't fathom leaving him with no one to greet. With the hopes that he would become part of another family, I took him to another Polyface satellite farm. Budhi and Gussy were tougher. I was certain they would survive our departure, so I decided to leave them. Carl and Norma promised to continue feeding them.

Considering what was next kept surfacing in our conversations, but without anything specific summoning us, we had to be patient. A lot of people assumed we would head back to California and we considered that option, but it was a long way back to the West Coast and too far away from my aging parents.

Joel invited us to manage other Polyface satellite farms. The idea was tempting, so we walked those rich fertile farms with him in hopes of feeling a connection to the terrain like we did when we interviewed for Buxton Farm. The other satellite farms weren't as beautiful as Buxton, but each one of them had a radiance. As appealing as it was to consider, we had to be honest that we weren't feeling inspired to shepherd any of his other rental farms. It was definitely time for us to move on.

When we moved to Buxton Farm, I brought boxes of journals I had accumulated over the years. Carting them with us to our next destination didn't seem necessary. So one rainy afternoon, I scanned through every entry and realized nothing I read felt significant to me anymore. I put all those journals inside Buxton's wood burning stove and as they went up in smoke I sensed a door to the past close.

Dear Kip, Dave, and Dick,   *11-11-2012*

We hope this note finds you well! The last two years have been quite a journey. A fantastic one. Moving to Virginia was a step in a promising direction for us. There aren't many places remaining that embody the small town exquisite wonder like Bath County. What a special place. Truly delightful. Michael and I wanted to live on land for several years, so in a way Buxton has been a dream come true. Our lives have always been focused around Mother Nature's gifts. Living on the land has been so delicious! We also enjoy bringing new life wherever we call home.

It's true we came across the country for the experience with Polyface. I don't think anyone else could have pulled us out and away from the vibrant life we had on the West Coast. When life gives you a "hell yes," it's hard to deny the eagerness and adventure new experiences bring. We wouldn't change a thing about our decision, but we must admit that when we first moved here we thought and hoped we would be here longer than two years.

The first year was a continual test of patience, courage, strength, and stamina. The second year we weren't as rusty! We felt like we created a smooth flow for the most part. Not to mention, we had wonderful people assisting us. So many things, people, and events made this opportunity at Buxton rewarding. We carry with us new skills and a whole new level of confidence about where we are headed. Somehow, we managed to fulfill personal and professional wishes during our two-year commitment in Virginia.

Living in the country gave us insight into simpler things in life, and also helped us better understand why it seemed something was missing living too remote. We're more socially inclined than we initially realized! In the end, it feels like things are always working out, and we feel certain things will come together for your beautiful farm as well.

We want to express our sincere appreciation to each one of you for allowing us to have our tiny studio on your land. We could not have survived without some privacy during the season. Our wonderful portable space restored our spirits. It's been a worthy investment!

We want only the best for the land, and for you guys, as you consider the next family to live at Buxton. We're certain things will come together. Thank you for being part of two very special years.

Be well,
Grace and Michael

We were offered opportunities to farm in Kentucky, New Mexico, Wisconsin, Pennsylvania, South Carolina, California, Virginia, Texas, Washington, Michigan, New York, Florida and several other states. It was fun sorting through the different options. After living in such a remote area for two years one of our highest priorities was to be within reach of culture, music, and diversity. We didn't think it was too much to ask, and we knew California wasn't our only option.

We made sure that old farmhouse was neat and clean when we closed it up. Even though the next tenants wouldn't be working with Polyface, I hoped someone special would pick up where we left off. We were halfway down the driveway when Carl pulled up in his old green truck to say goodbye. He was worried he was going to miss our departure. It's funny how things work out. When we first arrived at Buxton he kept us at a distance, but now it was hard for him to see us leave, and we felt the same way. I fell sobbing into his arms. It was likely we'd never see one another again. Michael and I never could have survived stewarding that land without his advice and knowledge of intimate details about Buxton. The exchanges we shared as friends over the course of two years were rich and powerful. That final farewell crystallized our departure. As we pulled away in our overloaded car, I knew it would probably be a long time, if ever, before I'd return to that untamed land. So much had transpired in two years at Buxton. I was leaving with a few new scars, something I didn't see coming when we arrived with so much anticipation from the West Coast. In a way, leaving Buxton was akin to another death in my life, another loss. But like other transitions, I knew our farewell preceded a wonderful new beginning: exciting opportunities are always waiting patiently around the corner for us.

Before we could figure out what was next, we needed time to reflect. Many years had passed since Michael's brother Jim was sent to prison. The time had come for Jim's release and Michael could hardly wait to see him. He headed to Texas to visit his family and I drove to Ohio, where my father's health was quickly deteriorating.

We're All Just Passing Thru

When I arrived at my parents' condominium, I was pleased to see Dad at home in his own bed with hospice nurses checking in on him. The last place he wanted to be, while he was dying, was in a stale hospital room, and the last place I wanted to be was thousands of miles away. Closure is a priority of mine.

Dad was born in 1924 to a mother he never knew and adopted by a family in Ohio. His adoptive mother yearned for a second child but kept having miscarriages. An aunt who worked for social services lived with Dad's adoptive parents and one night she brought a baby boy home; that baby was my father. To this day there's no record of my father's birth. It remains a mystery exactly where Dad came from, it's likely he was a black market baby.

I sensed my father's lack of trust in the world started when his real mother abandoned him, and he was raised by an older couple but never truly bonded with them. Maybe that was one reason he was hard to get close to. When I was growing up, he rarely showed affection, and his temper quickly went to rage. Often I walked on eggshells around him. Later in life, perhaps due to burying several of his children, he became softer, more approachable, sometimes even vulnerable. At the end of our phone conversations, he started to say "I love you."

The first time he saw Mom was in second grade, and he never took his eyes off her again. He claimed he was born married. Mom and Dad married young and had their first child before they were twenty. Despite their heated arguments over the years, my parents were at their best when they were together. For sixty-eight years, they were almost inseparable.

Throughout his life he was deeply devoted to the Catholic Church and rarely missed Sunday mass. He consumed up to six or eight cups of instant coffee a day, and because his gut was made of steel, he ate whatever he wished. He thought we were nuts spending money on bottled water, and claimed there was nothing wrong with the chlorinated tap water that came out of his kitchen sink. He drank it daily.

Visiting him now, he looked like a tiny old man in his king-size bed. His body was bone thin. With very little strength to get to the bathroom, we resorted to diapers and changed them frequently in an effort to keep him dry and comfortable.

He wanted to know what day it was, what the weather was like outside, where his daughters Erin, Pam, and Kerry were. He stared at Chelsey, his granddaughter's photo, on his mirror and wondered when she was coming home from Africa. From time to time, he thought he was on a boat. We assumed he was revisiting peak moments in his life, perhaps World War II days when he swept for mines in the Navy. A few times he asked me to open his closet doors and cabinets next to his bed because he thought people were hiding inside. Then he would ask for his wallet and check to see how much money was in it. He was certain someone was stealing from him. Every other day, he told Mom and me he wanted to go home. I knew what that meant, but Mom would respond with, "You are home." Then she'd turn up the TV so that the two of them could watch one of their programs. We made him as comfortable as possible in his final days. He preferred very little light, and not much interaction, but Mom kept waking him to eat his next meal, even though his appetite was gone. He ate for her, to please her. Whenever he would ask me how he ended up sick in bed, I'd smile and say, "You're old." Then he'd laugh and say, "You're right." Every time I was alone with him, I'd remind him it was okay to let go. "Just let go, it's okay, Mom will be fine." His blue eyes would stare into mine as he nodded his head in agreement, then he'd fall back asleep.

We decided to bring hospice in full-time because he began to lose consciousness. Michael and I stayed with him until a male nurse arrived for the evening shift. The nurse was unfazed by the circumstances, and settled into my parents' house as if it were his own. His presence was a relief to all of us. We knew Mom was in good hands, so we retreated to our room for some much needed rest. A few hours later, my sister Chris told us Dad died peacefully with Mom next to him.

The process of my father's death was profound and challenging, but I wouldn't have missed it for anything. It was the first death in my family that didn't feel tragic, untimely, or wrong. In fact, for me, his transition was natural and right. He lived a long, incredible life, and even though I knew I would miss him, I didn't feel any remorse or resistance about it ending. I felt certain once he let go, he would reemerge into another dimension where pain and suffering were nonexistent, and where he might be reunited with his own children, and perhaps even his biological mother, the woman he never knew.

The day we buried my father was bitter cold. The service was held in the same church where my sisters Amy and Kerry were married, Kim and Brian were buried, and where I once feared Catholic nuns. Just before the funeral ended, a very tall beautiful African-American man from the Navy played "Taps" on his bugle. He reminded us of our brother-in-law Blair, and we were comforted by his presence. That poignant military song was a beautiful ending to my father's long life. It was short and sentimental and my favorite part of the ceremony.

I credit Buxton Farm for the natural acceptance of my father's passage. On that farm I acquired an intimate understanding of the precious cycle of life and death. It's impossible to avoid in a farming lifestyle. Because we faced it almost everyday, when we left, I carried the notion with me: "We're all just passing through." It was a newfound revelation that I couldn't deny. Life on land in rural Virginia gave me the incredible gift of awareness that, no matter where you go, there you are; the internal landscape is really at the heart of living well, and the key is not in holding onto life, but embracing it with an open heart.

Runic Interpretation of Grace

Grace has runic energies signifying movement, wholeness, signals, journey, and partnership. She needs to travel and try on different points of view before she arrives at a sense of wholeness.

The Ansuz rune of signals helps her become more intuitive, and as she seeks balance in her personality, her limiting thought patterns are modified and Grace comes into balance. In time, Grace arrives at a state of well-being and joy. She no longer lives according to the opinions of others but seeks her own higher counsel.

((Excerpt from *The Hidden Truth of Your Name, A Complete Guide To First Names and What They Say About The Real You,* by The Nomenology Project)

Epilogue

Several years ago I felt a strong desire to change the name people know me by to Grace. I was a Permaculture student at the time sitting in class when the teacher introduced himself. He gave his birth name first, then his Muslim name. After his introduction an incredible rush of energy surged throughout my entire body, my face flushed, and then the name Grace lingered in my mind like an echo over and over and over. I had no idea where this name came from, but as we went around the classroom and introduced ourselves, I couldn't deny the overwhelming impulse to announce my new name. My logical mind was perplexed by this new identity and immediately wanted answers. Where did this name come from? Who is Grace? Why does this name feel so right? I felt suspicious of people who had the audacity to change their names and I considered the idea "airy fairy." I challenged the inner direction I was receiving, and thought, "What's the point of changing my name"?

Fortunately, the summoning of my new name was very strong and my efforts to disavow it were unsuccessful. I did some research and was surprised to discover that Ann, my middle name, is Hebrew and means "gracious," or "full of grace." In order for her children to be baptized in the Catholic church, Mom had to give me and my six sisters a Christian name. Since her middle name is Ann, she decided to keep it simple, and gave Ann as a middle name to each one of her seven daughters. As it turned out, I wasn't so far out in left field after all. At first, I was only halfheartedly committed to my new name, it took some time and an open mind to let Grace in. But as I did, I felt more and more at ease and in alignment with Grace.

I think we're all born with an innate sense of worthiness, vitality, well-being, and invincibility. The environment we're raised in fosters that birthright or diffuses it. Circumstances early in my life made re-discovering that intrinsic feeling of wholeness part of my path. Now that I've made peace with this aspect of my life story, I no longer feel burdened by the past. It is what it is. Making peace with it has liberated me, released me to tell a new story. The story of living aligned from a place of inspiration where instinct and intuition prevail, and where Grace is not only a name, but a state of being.

In 2013, Michael and I searched five months for the next place to call home. With a list of potential farms in mind we started out at Crane Dance Farm in Michigan, where we worked alongside Jill Johnson and Mary Willis and learned how to farrow pigs. We enjoyed two incredible and insightful months working with their sheep, cattle, poultry and pigs. Crane Dance Farm was the perfect transition from Buxton Farm.

Since we were within driving distance to Milwaukee, Wisconsin, we couldn't pass up an opportunity to visit Will Allen's urban farm, Growing Power. We had the privilege of meeting Will and working as volunteers with his well-informed staff. The contrast from farming in a rural setting to an urban environment surprisingly appealed to us. Growing Power's diversified dynamic solutions for providing food for people living in a food desert is remarkable.

From Milwaukee we traveled back to Virginia and stayed in our tiny studio on our friends homestead. Once again, our tiny private space came in handy! We considered managing a vegetable farm for a family owned restaurant in Abington Virginia, but when that opportunity didn't feel like a hell yes, we ventured to Kimberton, Pennsylvania where we worked on a Biodynamic dairy farm. Working intimately with diary cows intrigued us, but unfortunately not enough to feel relocating to Pennsylvania was our next logical step.

Moving some place unknown to us weighed heavily on our minds, and no matter how much I wanted to continue farming, my injured foot made committing to another farm questionable. With a specific list of desires at the forefront of our intentions, we remained open and patient. We followed the advice of a friend and visited western North Carolina. In between additional farming opportunities we returned to western North Carolina a second time. This time the lure of the mountains caught our attention.

After five months of searching for our new home, surprisingly we found it inside a city! I'm not entirely sure if we chose Asheville, North Carolina or if Asheville chose us, but moving there felt like our next "hell yes." The congenial people, the beautiful mountains, the diversity, and the vigorous energy of the city and forest so closely intertwined; all of it summoned us. Almost every person we interacted with on our visits was friendly and helpful. Immediately we felt at home.

Our first few nights sleeping in the city were shocking. The noise, cars, traffic, sirens, mowers, blowers, neighbors; all of the things we couldn't wait to get away from a few years earlier when we left the West Coast for rural Virginia, where right outside our front door, but we didn't resist them because there was something really right about choosing to live in the city. We got out of our cars and onto our bikes, and embraced the energy Asheville emanates. Although most people living with MCS consider cities one of the most challenging environments in which to live, I had no doubt my commitment to neuroplasticity and rewiring my brain would allow me to live wherever my heart desired. The seeds we planted at Buxton Farm for our next home blossomed. Our intentions to live within reach of culture, diversity, the arts, live music, local food and farmers, uplifting and open minded people were met. Day by day we have settled into our new environment. What follows us to western North Carolina is a surge of new energy, and the promise of our next adventure.

Suggested Reading

Everything You Need to Know to Feel Good by Candace Pert Ph. D with Nancy Marriott Hay House Inc. 2006

Three Simple Steps: A Map to Success in Business and Life by Trevor Blake, Benballa Books Inc. 2012

Choosing Easy World: A Guide to Opting Out of Struggle and Strife and Living in the Amazing Realm Where Everything is Easy, by Julia Roger Hamrick, St. Martins Press 2010

The Vortex: Where the Law of Attraction Assembles All Cooperative Relationships, by Esther and Jerry Hicks, The Teachings of Abraham, HayHouse Inc. 2009

Dying to be Me: My Journey from Cancer, To Near Death, To True Healing, by Anita Moorjani, Hay House Inc. 2012

Kitchen Table Wisdom: Stories That Heal by Rachael Naomi Remen, M.D., Published by the Penguin Group, Penguin Group Inc. 1996

Chelsey by Chelsey Shannon, Health Communications Inc. 2009

On Death and Dying, What the dying have to teach doctors, nurses, clergy, and their own family, by Elizabeth Kubler-Ross, M.D., Scribner New York NY 1969

The Human Machine A Trouble-Shooter's Manual Volume III, Hiatal Hernia Syndrome by Phil Selinsky, Orion Publishing 2012

Restoration Agriculture: Real-World Permaculture for Farmers, by Mark Shepard, Acres U.S.A 2013

The Blue Economy: 10 Years 100 Innovations 100 Million Jobs, by Gunter Pauli, Paradigm Publications 2010

Folks, This Ain't Normal: A Farmer's Advice for Happier Hens, Healthier People, and a Better World, by Joel Salatin, Hachette Book Group 2011

Introduction to Permaculture, by Bill Mollison with Reny Mia Slay, Tagari Publications 1991

City Chicks: Keeping Micro-flocks of Chickens as Garden Helpers, Compost Creators, Bio-recyclers, and Local Food Suppliers, by Patricia Foreman, Good Earth Publications 2010

Living Downstream: A Scientist's Personal Investigation of Cancer and the Environment, by Sandra Steingraber, Vintage Paperback, 1998

The One Straw Revolution: An Introduction to Natural Farming by Masanobu Fukuoka Rodale Press, 1978

Holy Shit: Managing Manure to Save Mankind by Gene Logsdon, Chelsea Green Publishing 2010

Radical Homemakers: Reclaiming Domesticity From a Consumer Culture by Shannon Hayes, Left to Right Press Chelsea Green Publishing Company 2010

The Vegetarian Myth: Food, Justice, and Sustainability by Lierre Keith, Flashpoint Press 2009

The Small-Scale Poultry Flock: An All-Natural Approach to Raising Chickens and Other Fowl for Home and Market Growers by Harvey Ussery, Chelsey Green Publishing 2011

The Fresh Honey Cookbook, 84 Recipes From a Beekeeper's Kitchen, by Laurey Masterton, Storey Publishing 2013

Little House On A Small Planet, Simple Home, Cozy Retreats and Energy Efficient Possibilities, by Shay Solomon, The Lyon's Press 2006

Portable Houses by Irene Rawlings and Mary Abel, Gibbs Smith, Publisher 2004

www.ingramcontent.com/pod-product-compliance
Lightning Source LLC
Chambersburg PA
CBHW030259290526
45785CB00001B/145